# MODES OF CONVERSATION

by Samuel

A study of humanity, conversation, and the fabric of reality.

Copyright © 2018 by Samuel Bagot

All rights reserved. This book or any portion thereof may not be reproduced or used in any manner whatsoever without the express written permission of the publisher except for the use of brief quotations in a book review.

First Printing, 2019

ISBN-13: 978-1-7331102-1-1

ISBN-10: 1-7331102-1-6

www.TheWakingLion.com

Don't fear death.  Fear not living!

- Samuel

# Contents

## Intro to the Field ............................................................. 1
- The Sun and the Moon .................................................. 1
- The Field of Modes of Conversation ............................. 3
- The Basic Premise ........................................................ 4
- What is a Mode of Conversation ................................... 6
- Components of a Mode of Conversation ...................... 8
- Observations on Talking Points .................................... 9
- The Beauty of the Field .............................................. 11

## Structure of the Field ................................................... 14
- Layout of the Field ...................................................... 14
- Through Life and the Field ......................................... 16
- Modes and People ...................................................... 17
- The Left and the Right ............................................... 18
- The Top and the Bottom ............................................ 22
- Summary of the Field ................................................. 26

## Walking Through the Field ............................................ 29
- Archetypal Placements ............................................... 29
- ~ Strata: Mainstream Entertainment and Vapid Escapism .................................................................. 31
- An Interlude to Sanity ................................................ 35
- ~ Strata: Tribal Escapism ........................................... 37
- Wasting Time .............................................................. 40
- Semi-Opposing Modes ............................................... 41
- ~ Strata: Politics ......................................................... 43
- Going Deeper ............................................................. 44
- Ultimate Draw of Conversation .................................. 46
- Consciousness and the Strata of Politics ................... 47
- A Warning About Politics ............................................ 55
- The Formation of Strata ............................................. 57
- ~ Strata: Leftism and Conservatism .......................... 59

~ Strata: Socialism and Republic ................................ 62
The Evolution of Conversations ................................. 69
~ Strata: Communism and Free Market ..................... 72
~ Strata:  The State ...................................................... 87
~ Strata: Collectivism and Individualism .................... 92
Looking Down and Looking Up .................................. 96
The Formation of the Columns .................................. 98
~ Strata: Religion and Spirituality .............................. 101
Where I Float ............................................................. 108
Other Religions .......................................................... 109
~ Strata: Pure Consciousness .................................... 111
To Be or Not to Be ..................................................... 113
Simplicity of Consciousness ....................................... 114

Reflection on the Field .................................................. 116
The Pillars Above ....................................................... 116
Hot and Cold Water ................................................... 117
Stepping Back ............................................................ 120
The Mode of You ....................................................... 121
Your Current Modality  .............................................. 123
Be Brave! ................................................................... 127

# Intro to the Field

## The Sun and the Moon

The Sun and the Moon come and go. The Sun comes out in the day, and the Moon comes out in the night. The pattern is day, night, day, night. However, we know the Sun is always somewhere right? We know it's always day somewhere. If we take a step back, we see that it's not as simple as night and day. There's only one long day. The day you find yourself in is the only day you'll see.

You talk to your friend, you talk to your coworker, and then you talk to your postman. And you converse with yourself in between. And you converse with yourself in between about the same thoughts you talked about with others. Have you ever noticed that the ideas you talk about bleed into conversations with different people throughout the day?

The same is true throughout life. Though we call them independent conversations, the day's conversations are really just one continuous conversation for that day. And as sure as all the days are the same day, all the conversations you'll have in your life are just one long conversation. And ultimately, it's a conversation that you have with yourself. Life itself is simply one long conversation that you have with yourself. Wherever you go, there you are.

# The Field of Modes of Conversation

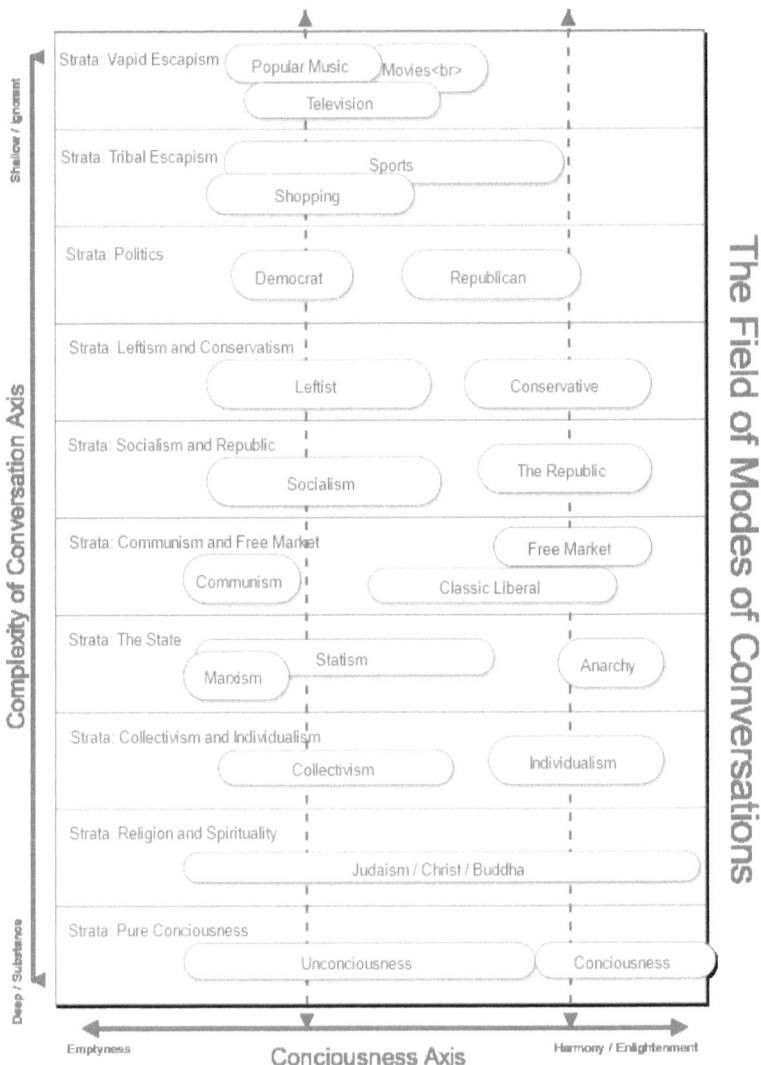

## The Basic Premise

These are some basic thoughts on the balance between different modalities of conversation a person moves through in life. The way that I visualize conversation between people is simple. They speak either on simple or complex subjects, and they speak either towards the goal of consciousness or from the slumber of unconsciousness. In order to observe this phenomenon, I place these two factors on a chart, which I call the field, and plot out different stances, which I call modes of conversation (MOC). Modes of conversation are nebulous groups of talking points from which a person may speak. I call the stance someone takes at any given time the modality of their conversation because, though they may identify with it, they're never fully invested or embodied by the stance. Their stance changes as they gain knowledge or because they become more conscious. It's simply the mode of their conversation at that time.

From what I've seen, people take different stances in life on different subjects. However, in general, they take a stance on life at large, and that stance informs most of their opinions on smaller issues. Their general stance on life can be approximated to an area of the field of modes of conversation. Around that area floats the talking points they currently utilize and their talking points nebulously clump together into their mode of conversation. The field is the laying out of every concept that can be declared or agreed upon.

I think a lot about how to gauge someone's general stance on life and where they currently are in the maze of philosophy. I've noticed that people's stance on life and thus their opinions on smaller subjects also changes throughout life. I see it as the natural progress of a soul through its adventure on Earth, and I want to celebrate that progression and reflect on it. I want to reason on the flow of conversation and not any specific conversation.

That is the mode of *this* conversation. Welcome. I want to unveil the evolution of modes of conversation and show that they can be observed and reasoned upon. The tool of my observation in this endeavor is the field of modes of conversation.

# What is a Mode of Conversation

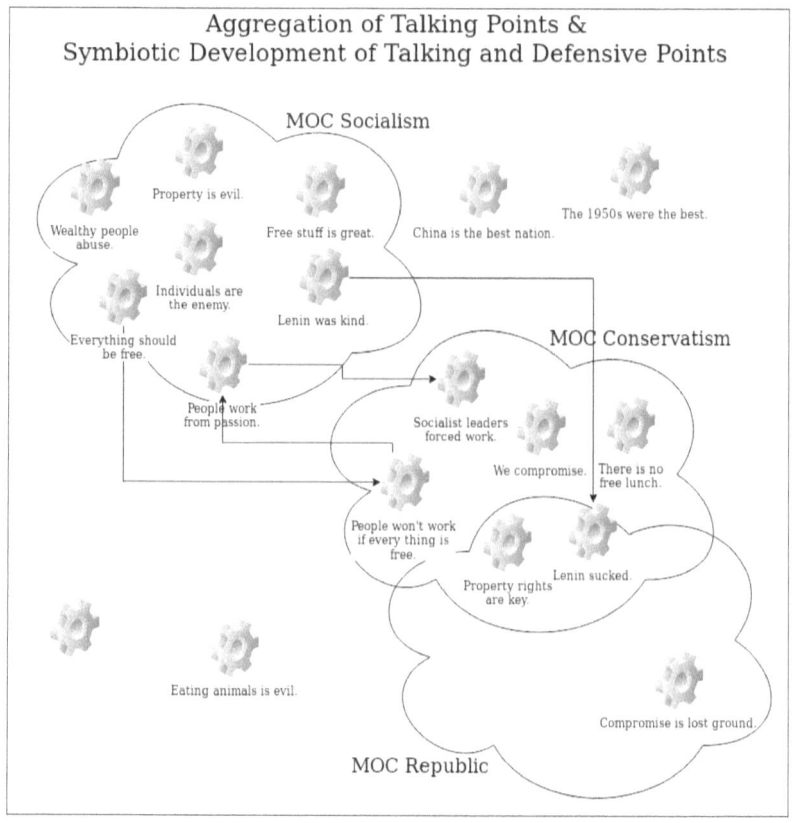

The way I see people adopting a stance on life is that they hear conversations, watch news, have people influencing them, and they self-reflect on events in their lives. They also to a large degree seem to pick their stance in life based off what benefits them socially and financially, though people typically never admit that such obvious factors may fuel their stance on aspects of life.  The basis of most people's stance on life is getting resources, either morally or immorally.  As they go through life, each person will formulate a combination of observations and ideas that they experience in some form or fashion.  They will speak from that stance as their mode of conversation.

This collection of observations and ideas formulate a set of agreements they then defend or speak out on, either to test their assumptions or to push for their personal benefit.  This behavior is what I'm referring to as speaking *from* a modality of conversation.  It's simply the mode of their current conversation.  It's the mode from which they speak which they will defend either rationally or irrationally with various psychological coping mechanisms.  The modality of conversation from which someone speaks guides the way they speak and the way they react in social situations.  A modality of conversation includes nebulously three components which are: a set of basic agreements, a set of talking points, and a set of defensive points.

## Components of a Mode of Conversation

- The set of basic agreements is simple a list of principles, beliefs, and faiths that are openly, secretly, consciously, or sub-consciously adopted.

- The set of talking points is a list of quotes, sayings, anecdotes, statistics, facts, pseudo-facts, etc., that a person can throw out as common claims for the given modality of conversation they're speaking from. These are the weapons they use and sharpen to get what they're seeking. These are the swords in the war of the minds.

- The set of defensive points is another list of quotes, sayings, anecdotes, statistics, facts, pseudo-facts, etc., that are available to quickly throw out in defense of known or well-established criticisms of the given modality of conversation. These are the shields and armor of the war in heaven. These defensive points will in many cases be simple responses to talking points of some other conflicting mode of conversation. They often develop symbiotically as other MOC develop.

## Observations on Talking Points

A given concept in a list of talking points or defensive points can be true, like a fact or statistic, but it's important to note that lists of talking points and lists of defensive points don't necessarily need to be accurate and optionally can even be completely baseless. These concepts can be a mix of fact and fiction. Their core psychological function is sometimes just conversational. Talking points are potentially sophistic in nature. They can be there to simply provide rationalization when another person questions the narrative of a modality of conversation. They can also be to simply have a response, empty or not, to volley the conversation back to a critic of a MOC. They can even be completely off topic but still conversationally advantageous as an attempt to change the subject.

Also, a potentially inaccurate talking point can be thrown out into a conversation as a rallying cry during group conversations when people of a particular mode of conversation feel that they can out number someone speaking from another MOC. Like a battering ram the group is attempting to push. In this case, truth isn't valued. The conversational purpose of such an inaccurate statement will be fulfilled as the larger group feels rationalization in numbers for what they are fighting for. This is basic primate pack mentality.

This is why texts like *Rules for Radicals* work so well. While destructive in nature, it's very effective. Saul Alinsky's epigraph in *Rules for Radicals* is very telling. The epigraph is gushing tribute to Lucifer for being a pied piper. It's a text book for mob manipulation and a complete abandonment of seeking truth. Trashy politicians love Saul for obvious reasons.

Empty sophism is a very powerful tool for those whose goal isn't truth and for those who have relative morals. Relative morals means simply choosing morality when it benefits the speaker. The ends justify the means in these conversations. So, talking points are sometimes just talking points and have no benefit to long term society.

Talking points used to support or defend a mode of conversation can also be simple truths, verifiable facts, or verifiable statistics as well. Seeking truth in life compels a person to speak more true concepts and purge fake concepts. It's pretty simple.

I'm just noting here that there's a mix of fact and fiction any time you're dealing with humans. Humans are emotional and rarely, if ever, data driven. And to make things more complicated, the most important decisions in life require resolution where no data is possible.

## The Beauty of the Field

So, back to the field of modes of conversation. It's a visualization of some of the different common, archetypal modes of conversation and where they are relative to each other conversationally. Also, one can observe how a soul passes through different stages of self-actualization by observing how conversation changes throughout a lifetime. I really do feel that what I've found is nothing short of profound and beautiful. Yet, I'm sure, it's nothing new. There's nothing new under the Sun.

Not only does the field accurately map my progression in life, give me direction, and show me purpose, I see many others around me following this flow of conversational progress as well. I see it as a deep and beautiful reflection on life itself. This is an observation whose time has come. It's a necessary step in our evolution because morality is an evolutionary tool. Morality and consciousness converge in time. They become the same thing, and we're finding that now. So, please help me formulate these ideas if you feel like helping out humanity.

# Structure of the Field

## Layout of the Field

The way that I picture the field of modes is a plane with a top/bottom axis and a left/right axis. At the top of the field I place shallower conversational modes that require less deep understanding and less knowledge or research.

At the bottom of the field I place conversational modes that require more research or deep reflection of the self. The top/bottom, vertical axis is the Complexity of Conversation Axis. How self-reflective and deep are your conversations?

On the left side of the field I place conversational modes which are less conscious, as in they require a sentient being to do less decision making, less cognitive work, or restrict the ability to express individual will. A repeat of that… less decision making by the individual. This is very important. The individual, of course, is the only component of existence capable of expressing will power. Will power is the building block of consciousness. Attacks on the individual or will power are symptoms of unconsciousness.

On the right side of the field, I place conversational modes which are more conscious, require self-determination, self-actualization, and more cognitive self-reflection work. The modes of conversation in the right area of the field promote the expression, flourishing, and strengthening of will power. After all, we're to choose our destiny. And to not decide *is* to decide not. The left/right, horizontal axis is the Consciousness Axis.

Someone could potentially see a reflection of the left/right paradigm of American or global politics inside the Consciousness Axis. I would note here that the world's made of humans and the macro will reflect the micro, but I'd encourage people not to directly impose simple politics on top of this field because they'll miss the point. The common leftist modality obviously firmly belongs on the left of the field of modes, but republicans, per se, don't necessarily fit completely to the right on this field.

Consciousness is the spectrum we focus on with the left/right axis and the field isn't a take on Democrat versus Republican. This field graphs Unconsciousness versus Consciousness and not political left versus political right. View this new field of modes with an open mind and you'll see the truths it unveils. This is important because the left/right political idea is usually a false dichotomy.

## Through Life and the Field

Obviously, as true in life, I see the progress of a human as moving deeper into more complex conversations throughout life, and thus downwards on this field of modes. I also see the spiritual progress of a being as going from less consciousness towards more consciousness... if they're fit. And this means towards the right on the field of modes. Fulfillment through self-actualization and expression of will are more prevalent towards the end of a person's life than initially in life if they move towards consciousness, as they normally do. We're built for that after all. This is the flowering of our minds. Our minds are the flowers in the garden. So, the general motion of a soul through life is down and right on the field. This is true of species as well.

## Modes and People

I typicality talk about these stances in life as modes, and I try not to address the people who adopt these modes directly. This is because the people themselves are not the modes. They're adopting these modes of conversation as a defensive mechanism to a world they fear. We're not going to be afraid anymore though. We're moving beyond all this, and you're going to love it. The modes are more like egos than true representations of a person. You aren't your ego, and you aren't your mode of conversation. Let it go.

People adopt these modes of conversations and memorize their talking points specifically because they haven't seen a better view of life yet. But there's nothing like a message whose time has come, and we live in an age where better ways to approach life are being revealed. We approach a time of more harmony, and the tumultuous nature of our lives is actually the sign of that. Remember modalities fight each other, and people are the conduit of those energies. And this energy flow is a market where people will move towards better ideas as they come along. Welcome to the present!

## The Left and the Right

It's like the saying goes: There are two kinds of people in the world; those who want to be left alone and those who won't leave them alone. The left/right spectrum of the field is called the Consciousness Axis. Observation of the Consciousness Axis really intrigues me. I see all humans' natural progression in life, and possibly the point of life as a motion to become more conscious. The path people take in the field is overwhelmingly towards the conscious side of the field when mapped out over the course of their life, if they're lucky. I don't believe in luck, of course. That's why I say "If they are fit."

I see increasingly unconscious conversation towards the left side and increasingly conscious conversation towards the right side of the field. I guess the far-right edge would be a singularity, asymptote, or to fully see all. I see the concept of separate objects as a mirage of smoke between the mirrors. Some call it the forms and the formless. That's a different conversation though. The Consciousness Axis scales from the left speaking of having other people make our decisions in life to the right speaking of making our decisions for ourselves. Also, as one would expect, by definition, if one is to accept that others should make our decisions, then they must also believe that there exists a person qualified to make decisions for others. In a deck of tarot cards, there's a card called The Fool that illustrates this situation.

The left side of this axis may speak more of heavy bureaucracies or that there should be some professional out there telling us what to do. Fear of consciousness is dangerous and evil people promote unconscious conversation because unconscious people are very "useful". The unconscious are less in control of their lives. This is because they demand to be less in control of their lives.

Some examples of being less conscious and not demanding your own will are

- Someone telling you what to eat
- How to work
- Where to work
- What you can say
- What you can't say
- If you should be able to defend yourself
- If you should even be allowed to live

The left side of the field loves the proverbial "they" who are idolized as the professionals. The evil proverbial "they" seek through the world, and unfortunately find, unconscious people to control and prey upon!

Modes on the right speak more about demanding that we make our own decisions in life. With that, these conversations tend less to demand control over others. The right-side modes speak from an attempt at consciousness which doesn't always make a perfect decision, but it does, however, seek to have a more cognitive component to life. They echo that people want to make their own decisions. A common theme is that people make better decisions for themselves and it's better to either benefit from the outcomes of our decisions or learn from our mistakes. This approach makes a better world long term as people are learning and collecting the "whys" on a personal level. They are learning why as an individual in a world where there is no forest, only trees. Life really is amazing in that it pushes people in the direction of consciousness. Self-actualization is the goal and self-reflection is the method.

The reason that consciousness is preferable in this progression, despite the possibility of mistakes, is that the mistakes are okay. They're okay because we're not here to build a perfect history or cure human error. We are instead here to build a Consciousness in tune with the Green Gift... a harmony... that knows why. It must know why first. It must seek. It must know why in order to arrive where It needs to be. It must make the decision consciously to move towards harmony and nothing else can make that decision for It. I am It by the way. You are It.

I picture harmony as a mind that moves in a certain way specifically because it's gathered the Whys that lead to harmony. Harmony can't be skipped to. The Whys have to be gathered first like sticks on the floor of a forest when you're starting a fire. I call the gathering of the whys Conscious Capital. People gather their personal whys slowly throughout life, and that's how, and why, people move from unconsciousness towards consciousness. This flow of an individual can be seen and charted on the field of modes of conversations and it's typically down and to the right. This is why it's said that if you're young and not more towards the left then you may have no heart, but if you're old and not more towards the right, then you're... Well, you have to find that out on your own, and you will. This movement across the field happens to individuals and entire species in the same way. Humanity's time has come. This is our species' time.

## The Top and the Bottom

Oscar Wilde said: "The Universe itself shall be our Immortality!" In his 1881 poem Panthea, Oscar Wilde chose to capitalize a very interesting set of words as being proper nouns including the word Universe. Any word in his poem that would refer to The Thing That Is is capitalized as proper and singular. The Greek word Panthea means "of all Gods" which is itself a reference to the Mono-Theism... The Thing That Is. He capitalizes these words for this reason.

The poem's also appropriately illusive to the moments of love between a man and a woman, which is the center of The Spiral and makes up the fabric of our existence. Life is a spiral of love and attraction between a man and a woman. Amazing, right? Smart guy. But I digress.

Back to the top/bottom spectrum. The Universe is our immorality as we have to make things on the physical plane to survive. We have to solve problems in the physical world to survive. We have to overcome physical obstacles to keep existing on this physical plane and in the Green Gift. The body is the temple of the soul and will. The body is the physical place, in the physical world, where your cognitive machinery exists. It must be maintained to keep your thoughts and your generations going... period.

The Tree of Life requires that you protect the temple. *The Thing That Is* can only be described as something that *Is* because, in Its decent into this physical plane, It has anchors which It wishes to maintain and spread.

We are those anchors and Its children. It loved the world so much that It wants and compels eternal life on this plane, and you are what It created to maintain Its existence here. You are Its joy. You are Its experience here. You are the soul point of Its vested interest here. And, you're a part of It.

We seek harmony on this physical plane and in the Green Gift. That is to say that we're seeking a way to survive here and to do so in such a way that we get to live out a fulfilling life as individuals. And we want to be assured that, forever into the future, our progeny can do the same. This is the Tree of Life. And I do mean forever. Life in this moment depends on the notion that life will never end. Our minds don't work correctly unless we feel this way about our world. This means avoiding harm, danger, extinction, etc… forever. Balance! We seek to keep the flower in full bloom.

In seeking the solutions to the problems on the physical plane and balance of resource usage that will provide forever without overpopulation, we must observe the physical world. We must build things like water pumps, food production, transportation, economic systems, medical technology, etc.

Developing these things requires an increasingly deep knowledge of the physical world and reflection on *What Is True*, or more specifically *The Thing That Is*. Subject matters must be studied, articulated, and reasoned on.

So, our people and our species must become increasingly involved in more complex and deeper subjects within the Green Gift. We can't sit around and talk about football and shopping and expect to overcome a famine or an asteroid that comes our way. We're not guaranteed tomorrow on the Green Gift. That's why it's a gift. It's just an offer. This is the nature of the top/bottom axis and it's appropriately named the Complexity of Conversation Axis.

Simpler conversations with lower "barrier to entry" are towards the shallower top, and deeper in the field are the more complex and deeper conversations. The subjects of deeper conversations don't have to be physical but can be. Those conversations can be conceptual like economics which reflects on and forms physical systems. Those conversations can also be more concrete like rocket science which yields stronger rockets.

We as individuals are encouraged to add to the progress of our species and study something worthwhile to contribute to the struggle of mankind. I've heard it said that there is a special place in Hell for sports fans.  My friends are going to complain that I said that but stick with me for a second.  Sports are cool, but don't get stuck on any one conversation, because we DO have to find the way to "forever" inside Its Green Gift.  I accept the gift and the challenge.  Remember, our destiny and personal responsibility is to know that we're here to build a Consciousness in tune with the Green Gift. To build a harmony that knows why.  We must dive deeper into the more complex subjects to find the physical "whys".

## Summary of the Field

So that's the field of modalities of conversation.  It's a consciousness scale and a complexity scale.  The field can be used as an observational tool to help people reflect on their ideas, assumptions, and progress throughout life.  As you can see, I focus on the individual because the individual is the expression of humanity and the only creation capable of thought. Specifically speaking, collectives don't have thoughts and can't make decisions.

The individual is the Temple of the Will just as the body is the Temple of the Soul. The individual is the application point of all philosophy, virtue, and principle. The individual is the creation in which What Is has placed the responsibility of seeking truth and What Is. The truth... *is* the truth. The individual is also the only creation that is capable of experiencing the fulfillment of seeking truth and What Is. Seeking consciousness must focus on the individual and that process is called self-actualization.

The field, in that same spirit, is much more useful as a tool for the individual to reflect on their own mind and isn't always useful as a tool for people to evaluate others. It's also a useful tool for reflecting on the direction of your nation or species as a group of conscious individuals. There's no forest. There are only trees. Applying the principles learned from this field will naturally create a more open society and require less regulation. The main principle being that we should always push deeper and towards consciousness.

# Walking Through the Field

## Archetypal Placements

Throughout the field I drew in the book, I sprinkled some of the more commonly known MOC as sign posts on the mapped field. As you can see, the modes that I placed on the field are more archetypal in nature. People adopt them as they perceive them to be beneficial. You may not agree with my specific placement of some of these modes of conversation, but I currently do. And it doesn't matter because the principle behind the field exists beyond any argument that would take place over the placement of any specific mode.

Don't get caught up on the placement of your favorite MOC. The placement of a mode matters less than the general theory of the field, and people travel through the modes as life goes on anyway. Adopting a mode of conversation has more to do with learning its talking points, defense points, and claiming it as an identity than it does actually becoming modality. You aren't the modality. You aren't your ego, right?

Next, I'll traverse a general walk-through of some archetypal modes of conversation and why I placed them on the field as I did in relation to each other. I'll outline some modalities that seem to oppose each other and what that means in their execution and evolution. I'll also identify some strata of MOC that I see existing along the vertical Complexity of Conversation Axis.

# ~ Strata: Mainstream Entertainment and Vapid Escapism

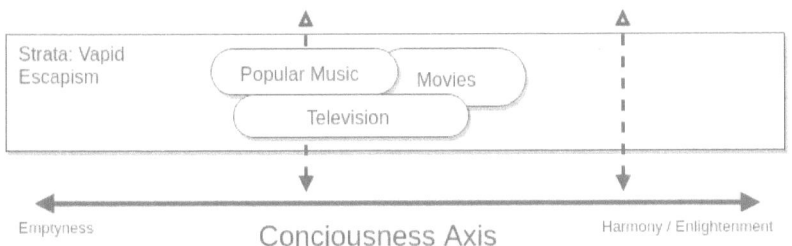

Towards the top there exists the shallower modes of conversation that people can speak from. This means lower "barrier to entry" conversation and generally involves more infantile concepts. Of course, not every conversation has to be a gruelingly harsh introspection, but these modalities of conversation and the shallow nature of this area of the field is important to understand.

I see entertainment towards the top in general. Most forms of modern entertainment are just escapism. The conversations that most forms of modern entertainment produce are quite empty. When was the last time someone said something awe inspiring that they found through reflecting on the latest episode of any modern show? It doesn't happen.

Most television shows, popular songs, movies, etc., are simply vapid escapisms that generate only meaningless or self-indulgent conversations. I've noticed for a while now that people often apologize for bringing up modern movies or television shows in conversations because those forms of entertainment have become so embarrassing. A friend may say "I know it's a dumb show, but I've watched a lot of it." People call shows guilty pleasures sometimes. The guilt, of course, comes from the shows being wastes of their time and they know it.

These forms of escapism tend to mask both the pain and beauty of raw life and break the dynamic nature of interesting conversation. An example would be someone without anything interesting to say because they're obsessed with popular culture and constantly escaping their own adventure. They would never develop their own adventure. Modern movies and Hollywood in general attempt to completely separated us from our amazing ability to self-reflect in their sad attempt to wag the dog. We're well into the era of being better off to avoid all mainstream movies, music, and television forever.

Escapism leads to less cognition and less consciousness. I'm thinking reality TV shows, cultural exploitation music, music award shows, Hollywood in general, etc. Also, the comedy news shows are particularly geared to help us check out mentally. The notion of this Entertainment is to choose to go on autopilot or to fill our boredom. It dulls our reflective energy which would normally be expressed as engaging conversation. It masks what would be a beautiful life with stories of fake characters' adventures.

Here, I'm commenting on the conversations around these forms of escapism. The conversations are equally vapid. I get it. Sometimes you have to blow off some steam, but in general being obsessed with shows, music, and movies will show through when we are speaking with others. If you like watching videos to cool off, documentaries and how-to videos are a step up from basic entertainment and will make our day to day conversations and self-reflection more dynamic.

The topics of vapid escapism prevent depth of conversation and can be easily assigned to the Complexity of Conversation Axis. They are shallow. Also, another danger of mainstream entertainment escapism is that other people are infusing their opinions and manipulations into the presentations. By doing so, entertainment icons degrade the general MOC of the populace. The music industry is particularly manipulative and evil.

It's very difficult to find mainstream entertainment without a manipulative message. We don't have to listen to them and we don't need to turn our brains off. We don't have to succumb to emotional pleas by mass sources of bias. We all know that mainstream entertainment makes a person foolish. The thing to notice as far as the field is that mainstream media dulls the quality and depth of the conversation you're capable of having with the world around you. It dulls the conversation you have with yourself. The Mainstream Entertainment and the Vapid Escapism strata are a danger to our species.

## An Interlude to Sanity

Think about something here before I continue. Did anything I just said bother you? Reflect on something for a second. You aren't your ego, and I'll be walking through some modes of conversation that you may think identify you. The notes I make about the conversations around some of these areas of the field are simply notes on the conversations in that area of the field. We sharpen each other through conversation and exchange of ideas, and I need your help with that. I'm sharpening myself. Don't take things personally. I need you to be strong in that way so that we can figure something out here. Respect is mutual.

In that light, I need you to view the field as if you weren't on it, because you aren't. I need you to view the field as if you didn't identify with any of the modalities of conversation that I'll mention. This is because the notes here don't apply fully to the people speaking from these modes of conversation. Let us not try the same things over and over.

We have to forgive all people who speak from any given mode of conversation for the ills we perceive in order to make progress ourselves. This is because it's the only way we can forgive ourselves when the time is right. It's the only way for us to step away from our identified modes of conversation and shed the ego. I suggest that we not attack, label, or pigeonhole anyone around us for speaking from a particular MOC. That forces an agreement deep within the attacker's mental dynamic that people's minds are set in stone. And that agreement will set the attacker's mind in stone instead. The human mind is fluid and shifting.

So, if you find yourself getting mad as you see me go through these modes of conversation, you may just be heavily or emotionally bound to one of them as an identity. You may be bound to an identity which may not always server you. My suggestion is that if you find yourself insulted in these observations of conversations, then just keep reading, and see if you can ultimately see this as just a dance towards a larger philosophical offer at the end of this conversation. Remember, there's a larger philosophical offer here.

## ~ Strata: Tribal Escapism

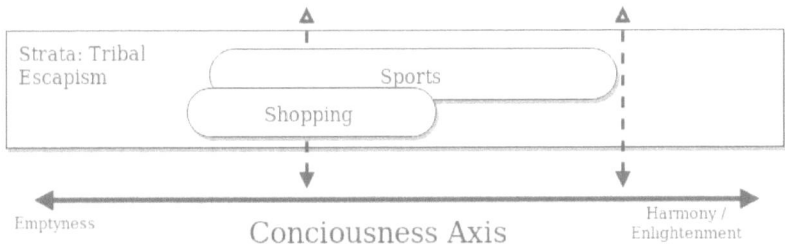

Right below the Vapid Escapism strata, you'll find the conversational area around sports, shopping, fashion, and other tribal forms of escapism. Social media is a tribal thing for some people and conversation through social media and texting is typically quite shallow. I put the interlude to sanity right before this one because people are particularly emotionally invested in sports and fashion, and it gets out of hand.

It's very rare that a person can only talk about sports or fashion. So, I'm not assuming that someone who talks about sports has no other dimension to their personality. I'm just noting that conversations around sports and fashion are pretty basic. People are multifaceted, so I definitely don't want to paint people that talk about sports or fashion as fools or idiots. The conversations these subjects derive are toward the top side of the Complexity of Conversation Axis.

Playing a sport is a different story but can still be obsessed over. I personally think that there should be more emphasis on dance and playing local sports, but that's not what I'm talking about here. Watching sports in general is just a form of escapism and reminds me of a person on a hamster wheel running from themselves. These conversations surround memorizing stats, memorizing plays, memorizing seasons, and memorizing the general science of how games are played. Shopping and fashion conversations are quite similar. Look up makeup tutorials on YouTube. It's seriously uncalled for. I'd go so far as to say that it's positively daft.

Conversations in this general area of the field could be argued to be complex, yet surprisingly applicable to nothing in life. However, I do see conversing about sports as a basic biological rallying activity of the pack nature of mankind, and I do actually think that's pretty important. This is why I put them in their own strata of Tribal Escapism. Fashion is tribal in that it's basically human sexual selection acting out its desire for youth and fertility especially in demographics that benefit from that pursuit.

So, some of this tribal nature is understandable, but in actuality, we're fairly intelligent at this point in history and we could choose any number of other subjects to talk about.  I'm a pack animal, and I see that as a positive trait.  I'm the most tribal person I know actually.  My pack is the humans and we serve the Tree of Life.

The positioning of the conversational modes in this strata is only to note that these subjects don't demand particularly deep levels of introspection.  They don't require a vast amount of research to drone on about for hours and years on end.  Talking about sports is like obsessing over the victories of others.  Why not just go play basketball with your family?  It's like television where there's basically no show that's worth talking about.  Yet there are television shows where people just sit around and talk about other television shows.  How valuable are those conversations to us?  They have no value and that's what I'm talking about here.

And fashion conversations remind me of the Beautiful Ones from John B. Calhoun's rat experiments. Makeup sadly reminds me of chasing youth by people who were lied to or wish to lie to others. There's a biological aspect there that we more or less aren't allowed to talk about, so that's that. I always wondered what fairer meant.

I've never fully understood the point of conversations in the fashion and fake allure area of the field. Keep in mind I'm focusing on the conversations in this area of the field and not the people. Stay focused on that please; it's important! Conversations in this area of the field typically remind me of diving head long into the irrelevant. I do like playing basketball though.

## Wasting Time

The devil doesn't have to steal your soul if you simply just waste your time voluntarily. Some pursuits are like a hamster wheel for your brain. You can memorize the stats and talk with people at the gym. Then you can speak about all these different little notes and statistics you memorize indicating how good you are at analyzing a game. But in general, there's no reason to have ever done any of that. Everyone has their hobbies though.  Conversations in this area have to be psychologically rationalized.  Playing a sport with friends or for health is one thing, but watching sports constantly is totally different.  And high-end fashion is a blatant neurosis.

Your time is very valuable, so be very wary of those asking for it with shinny lights.  Make no mistake; life is what you make it.  I've found that people of high self-respect typically treat their time on Earth as the main commodity.  Notice how much control sports, shopping, and Hollywood has over our lives.  That's not a coincidence.  Shallow conversation is required for this loss of control.  Entertainment and escapism modes of conversation lean farther towards the unconscious side of the field.

## Semi-Opposing Modes

A little bit farther down the field you can see some semi-opposing MOC being observed.  We would typically claim these are opposites in society.  They should never be confused with right versus wrong.  The process of consciousness deriving our life decisions is what will ultimately be what we find to be "right".  Unconsciousness creates confusion and is clutched to out of fear. In the end, decisions from less consciousness will be correctly identified as "wrong" or whatever invalidation term you may choose to utilize.

## ~ Strata: Politics

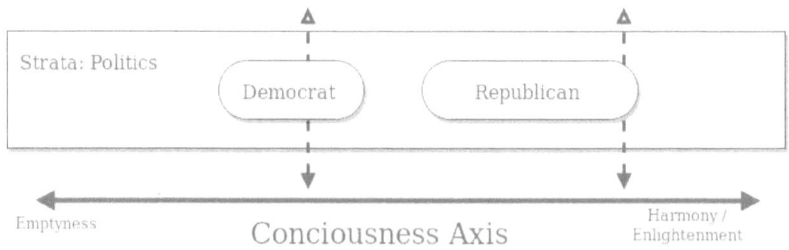

The first semi-opposing modalities we'll observe on the field are the MOC Democrat and the MOC Republican. This mainstream political strata floats towards the top of the Complexity of Conversation Axis, as you can see. These modalities are fairly low "barrier to entry". The talking points and defensive points for the modalities in this strata are passed out like fliers.

However, despite its shallow nature filled with unaware followers, this is an important strata and area of the field. People currently accept mainstream politics as the formation point of governments. Inside this area of the field lies the conversations that we believe formulate public policy.

The reason that the political strata is toward the top is because while it seems applicable to our society, it's mostly like a sport at this conversational level. For instance, one can adopt conversational modes in this strata despite having no understanding of the economy. This is a nightmare and terribly flawed. It's as common as dirt though.

There are, however, underlying philosophical modalities that are deeper, but they aren't always fully understood by people speaking in this strata. The Strata of Politics. We will discuss the underlying deeper MOC soon. Again, notice how I'm referring to *speaking* from these modalities and not *addressing* the people themselves. Most people that speak heavily from these areas of the field simply haven't ventured any further but soon will.

## Going Deeper

We will learn to go straight to the deeper underlying modalities and skip over the shallower modalities in the evolution of our understanding of the field. The political modalities, without understanding the deeper modalities and consciousness in general, are simply my team versus your team conversationally. They are interesting though because you can see the echoes of their deeper evolutionary roots even when the speakers don't understand the deeper roots. For example, the Democratic MOC is directly based off Communism/Collectivism and the Republican MOC is based off the Republic/Free Market/Individualism.

These deeper modalities aren't always directly referenced from shallower modalities, but are echoed. Ultimately, it's the deeper philosophical modalities that should be spoken from. A part of our self-actualization is to dig deeper and push downward in the field. Typically, people who haven't dug any deeper must be spoken with on their level. Once that's established, one has the option to carefully pull them deeper and to the right. Communication requires identification with what's being said. And there starts the game. There starts our battle. The battle is between two eternal forces which pull your mind either shallower and to the left or deeper and to the right. There two forces fear and love for the Tree of Life.

## Ultimate Draw of Conversation

Spoiler alert: Ultimately, people should be drawn towards talking about consciousness and towards focusing on consciousness. There isn't a long-term reason to deal in Democrat or Republican talking points or speak from those MOC. If you're stuck in shallower strata like these too long then your civilization is probably dying. But sometimes people are stuck there and must be talked to on the intellectual level they're comfortable with. Shallow conversation is basically only compelled by evil people to control less evolved people or as an opportunity by angels to draw someone deeper and towards more consciousness. You'll find which one you are soon enough. You'll soon know exactly what I'm talking about.

You'll always be lightly pulling into deeper conversation and more consciousness when you care about the person you're talking to. Either way, it's much more interesting to talk about the lower deeper modalities. So, you'll probably end up there out of boredom anyway.

It feels like plucking a guitar string when a shallower talking point is supported by a notion from a deeper modality. People just feel it and they don't even have to know why. It's compelling. Ultimately, we will utilize deeper philosophies to inform decisions made in shallower MOC, and I'll give some examples of that throughout. Mixing deeper modalities like Free Markets into the Republican modality is a much more potent message. Just like mixing Marxist Doctrine with modern day Democratic talking points.

## Consciousness and the Strata of Politics

The Democrat modality, as you can see, is farther towards the left side of the Consciousness Axis. The Democratic MOC include desire for less control over our lives and for decisions to be handed over to large government bureaucracies in exchange for getting free stuff more or less. Conversations in this area of the field typically loop endless talking points and rationalizations for less decision making and less responsibility by the individual. It also includes what has become a tidal wave of defensive victimization claims.

Any attempt to criticize the Democratic modality is now met with the immediate shield of avoidance of any and all responsibility via claims of victimhood.  This is the universal defensive talking point in this area of the field.  It's an unignorable phenomenon on the entire left side of the field.  It certainly wasn't as pervasive in the 80's and 90's but has blossomed into quite the looping record.  Its avoidance of personal responsibility pushes it farther towards the unconscious side as no person can control something which they claim they're a victim of.  Personal responsibility requires that you have a part to play and aren't helpless.  Consciousness and acceptance of control go hand in hand.

Also, intrinsic to the plight of life on Earth is a person accepting the ultimate responsibility of family and guiding children.  The modalities towards the left side of the field, including the Democratic MOC, contains a multitude of rationalizations for the loosening and denunciation of family.  This includes different conversations around not raising one's own children.  Denouncing the family structure is a direct attack on the Tree of Life.

By family structure, I mean the alignment of a male, a female, and a produced child. I call it the Triad of Life.

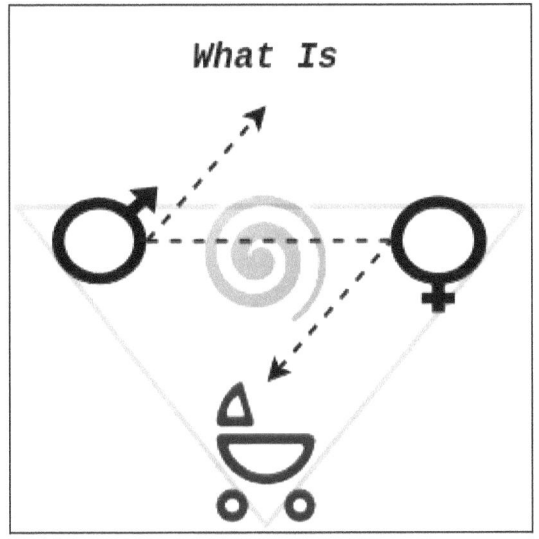

The Triad of Life

Each Triad of Life is linked two other Triads in that the male and female are the children of two other Triads. This looping pattern of beings I call the Crystalline Structure of Life.

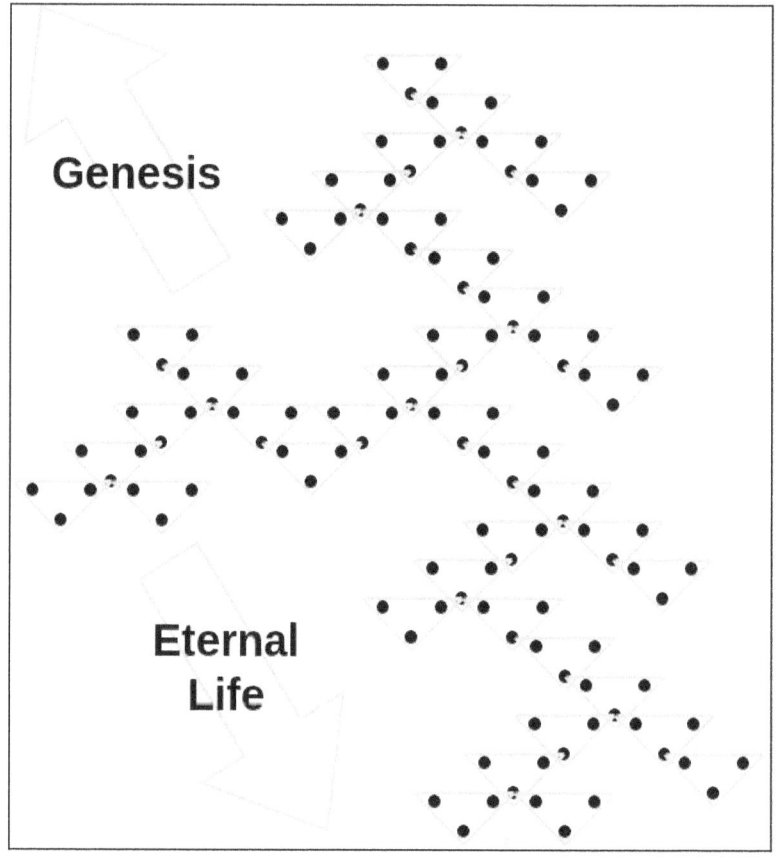

The Crystalline Structure of Life

Attempts to damage or loosen the Triad and family structure degrades the Crystalline structure of Life. Solid crystals are stronger, and weak crystals are more susceptible to cracking or shattering. If the crystalline Structure were to weaken enough, that branch would wilt and we would move into a spiritual phase called "first death", or Hell, followed by extinction. Remember, Life is just an offer to you. I choose Life.

The Tree radiating with energy, but never consumed.

Unconsciousness, as we'll find, produces a fear of defending the Triad of Life, which is the male/female/child metaphysical core of our existence's Crystalline Structure. People speaking from the Democratic MOC typically use what they may claim to be shared social responsibility to avoid having to raise their own children. Talking points about single parenthood are prevalent around these areas of conversation.

Talking points here iterate the belief that the state regulated public education system should teach our children how to think and what morals are. This area of the field contains many conversational attempts to rationalize letting the state completely raise our children. Some people even talk about children being state property. These manipulations are so prevalent in modernity that people rarely know what hit them. Many people speaking from the left side have an agreement that they aren't responsible for teaching their own children morals.

An example is the claim that it's beneficial to have nannies and day care raise our children. I guess, today, it's possible that the day care cares more about some children that the children's parents. This is a great point of contention in our society. It's ultimately ironed out when one digs deeper into the more complex modalities and then looks back up. Basically, all concepts seem complicated when confined to their own strata. A core principle of the field is that shallow areas look much clearer when you're looking upward from a deeper, more conscious area of the field. That's why digging deep is valuable.

The talking points adopted when speaking from the Republican MOC aren't completely conscious, of course. Conversations in this area of the field typically carry the shallow nature of the entire political strata. Relative to the Democrat MOC, the Republican MOC is typically not so based on modernity. It includes conversations more central to the family looking towards itself for answers. For instance, it provides rationalizations for private school, home schooling, and mothers staying at home to care for their children. This is, of course, an echo of some more deeply rooted philosophical modalities which speak of self-actualization. Towards the right, more conscious, side of the field, you'll see more conversations and talking points around self-actualization.

Self-actualization produces desire to raise one's own children as children are the most important of all self-actualizations. Our progeny is the focus of the Triad. The Triad is the focus of the Tree of Life. Conversations in this area are angled at a government which should do less for the people. Although on a shallow level, to speak from this modality is to believe in the natural order of the universe, which we find more and more every day to simply be the biological order of the Triad and the Tree.

The same can be said of all conversations around the right side of the field. Consciousness and cognition *are* the seeking of *What Is True*. That will always lead to and transcend biology. As expected, being a shallower echo of some deeper modalities, the Republican MOC doesn't always follow its deeper-rooted modalities. If one followed the tenants of the deeper modality completely, the person would simply be speaking from the deeper MOC. Also, Republican MOC certainly isn't a guarantee of consciousness and can be spoken from out of complete ignorance.

For instance, sometimes Republicans talk about needing bailouts and bigger bureaucracies. They failed to abolish the Department of Education which was a big part of why Reagan was elected. Republican conversation often defends interventions into other countries which entangle us in strange ways. I do believe in defensive war though. Democrats conversations do the same, but claim government intervention solves all problems.

The existence of Republican talking points rationalizing massive bureaucracy is simply an example that it's just another conversational phase a human goes through as it floats towards consciousness. So, don't stop at the Republican MOC, and don't get caught on those talking points. There are a great many unconscious agreements made by people speaking from the Republican MOC, and that's why it isn't placed on the complete right side of the field.

## A Warning About Politics

They say never talk about politics at a party. People are really sensitive here so don't try to talk someone out of their modality or interface them unless you know they're mature enough to have a mature conversation. Rattlesnakes are very dangerous when they're shedding because they can't see, and they'll attack anything around them that moves. The point of the field isn't to rationalize any endeavor supported by modalities like the Democrat or Republican modalities. Remember, real people are only speaking from these MOC. They'll flow out of them like hermit crabs when the time is right.

I've traveled most of the field myself, and I fully understand now that people drift. Most, if not all, the strong Republicans, and even Free Market economists, talk about how they read Marx and spoke from the Communistic MOC when they were in college. They're better now, of course. A great example of this is Thomas Sowell, the great libertarian economist. He was once a Marxist and even published a dissertation of Pro-Marxist views.

The field is a tool for reflection and not attack. So, don't tattoo any of these labels on others or nail them to their crosses. You'll have enough trouble dealing with your own cross when you decide to abandon your ego. Be ready. Real, live people typically flow into deeper conversation and towards the conscious side of the field throughout their life. And that's what it's all about ladies and gentleman.

## The Formation of Strata

As you'll see, I'm lining some modalities into strata to show the nature of dueling semi-opposing modalities and to help picture the way that modalities argue with each other. Major dueling archetypal modalities have talking points and defensive points that reciprocate each other because they evolved in symbiosis with each other. Just like consciousness evolved from unconsciousness and active from reactive. That's why symbiotes can be somewhat sectioned off into time periods. Evolution of conversation is chronological.

For instance, no one argues from the MOC of the Whig or the Tory anymore. And I don't bother to note them on the field, but they can be placed on the field as can all conversational modes. Although I know very little about those modes of conversation, I'm sure they were scales of consciousness. I'm sure one was for more self-actualization, and the other was probably for more safety through systemization of decision-making processes. Just a guess. I did read that those names were originally derogatory terms formed from arguments in the $17^{th}$ century about secession. Pretty indicative of conversations debating self-actualization if you ask me.

Fact check that if you want. I didn't care enough to iron out the Whig versus Tory conversation for complete relevance here. Any given semi-opposing modalities are nebulously opposing at best, and not necessarily perfectly opposing each other. These are just visualizations so you can see the engine under the hood when people are talking to each other and bickering. People are just adopting these MOC to attempt survival like a branch bending towards sunlight.

## ~ Strata: Leftism and Conservatism

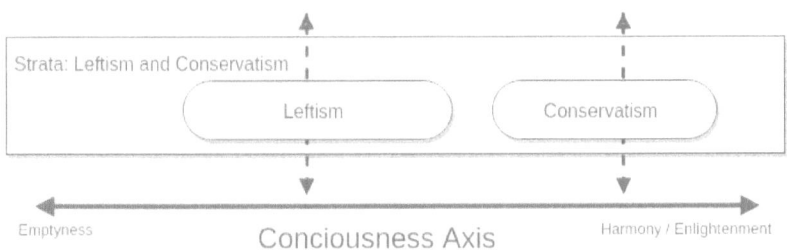

The next strata is Leftism MOC and Conservatism MOC. Note: I reserve the term Liberal for classical Liberal which is actually Libertarian in America. Also, in America, Liberal means someone on the political left which is a high-jacked term from the European Liberals which are referred to as Classic Liberals in America. This is confusing, so I don't say Liberal in this conversation. I didn't put Liberal on the field; I put Leftist. Also, Leftist in this case means left side of the American political scale and not specifically left side of my field of modalities, although they do coincide. This is an important idea to note because we as a species will soon abandon the left/right political paradigm and adopt something like this new field approach because it properly graphs out unconsciousness and consciousness. This field ultimately points us back towards the Triad of Life and greater human destiny.

And as you can tell, Democrats mode of conversation is derived from the modes of conversation of Leftism. Republicans MOC, in this same way, come from talking point of Conservatism. Conservatism means something a little bit different than Republican, doesn't it? However, it's easy to see how the Republican MOC and talking points are derived from conservative talking points. That's why they're placed close together on the field like this. Republican MOC is derived from Conservative MOC in ways.

The Democratic MOC in the same way is derived from a deeper belief in Leftism. People in the Leftism area of the field tend to speak about redistribution of the fruits of people's work and other collectivist ideas but don't necessarily have to subscribe to the notion that Democrats specifically are helping. As such, they may not vote for Democrats or may claim that they have no faith in the two-party system.

I like the term "derived from" because it shows a relationship but not a perfect copy. I also like to think about conversational modes as echoes of each other. To be "derived from" means they share some of the same talking points and can use some of the same defensive points. They have slightly different natures and slightly different opinions which differentiates the derived child MOC from the parent MOC, but they're pretty close to each other.

Understanding the mode of conversations of Conservatism really helps someone understand and identify with the talking points in the Republican MOC, right? You can see that same relationship with the Democratic MOC and the Leftism MOC. They're not the exact same and don't necessarily complete each other, but you can tell the relationship. In this light, some people in this area speak directly from the Leftism MOC and others speak directly from the Democratic MOC. Also, some people in this area speak directly from the Conservative MOC and others speak directly from the Republican MOC. Note how people push more into the political strata like Republican MOC and Democratic MOC around election time even if they don't identify as either side and may not even vote.

## ~ Strata: Socialism and Republic

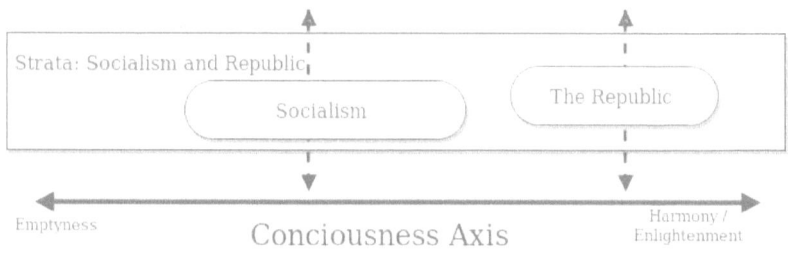

One strata down appears an older conversation which is the Socialism MOC and the Republic MOC. Again, this is where I place these for learning purposes, and these aren't the best examples of opposites. The last loops of conversations in this area were more in the 1940s and 1950s. People then learned a lot about humanity when experiencing mobs of people stuck in these modalities and the policies they created. Now society is completely ill-educated when it comes to the lessons that our grandparents learned and rightly fought against for survival. I said 1940s and 1950s, of course, because they found out the hard way about Socialism from Hitler. People apparently forgot the lesson of Hitler's Socialism very quickly and Socialism is back on the rise.

American actors and Academics in the 1990s ushered in and praised Chavez in Venezuela when he used the same talking points. Now that conversation has brought Venezuela into complete social break down and to the brink of cannibalism. Venezuela is done and could take hundreds of years to recover, if ever. Very sad. But the collapse of modern nations into complete disarray within a generation really does display the power of the Socialism MOC. It displays why we must take a step back to make sure we aren't talking ourselves into certain suicide around election time.

Evil is real. As we speak, there are elections here in America and around the world where candidates pour Socialist talking points onto desperate people and invite them into the roach motel. I say that not knowing the date you're reading this because this encroachment of evil is present in every election by nature. You may even be reading this from a time when unconsciousness completely collapsed America. You may have even just turned to this page as you scan the pages of this book before you throw it on a burning pile of books to appease a screaming mob.

Socialism/Communism/Unconsciousness is a skull staring you in the eyes and life turns out to just be an offer. Life owes us nothing. Life isn't promised. Life isn't guaranteed. If life doesn't bring you to your feet, then it will bring you to your knees.

The Socialism MOC focuses on an assumption that the main problem in life is that people have different outcomes when they make different choices. The conversation in this area of the field always draws towards forced equal outcome as the solution to all problems, and cracking a few eggs will be required. Here, all value should be redistributed and private property should be illegal.

Also, there's a lot of doctrine here pertaining to assertions of how the means of production should be public. This is now understood as government/elite ownership of all property and resources. To me, the word doctrine just indicates massive volumes of ideas that one would memorize to utilize later in a conversation to establishing credos. It's usually overly technical and thick. The main purpose of doctrine is to ensure that the speaker appears as an authority or to feign expertise. Social sciences are typically doctrine based.

The strangest aspect of conversations in this area of the field is that there are people buying control over the government which in turn write laws to force us to behave in certain ways.  This is then mistaken for problems with free will.  The left side of the field commonly seeks to prove that there is a problem with free will.  It's said that if we are allowed our have free will, then evil people can force others to do things against their own interests.  This is the typical frame of a "capitalism is evil" approach.  Therefore, the flow of these conversations eludes to "people shouldn't have free will."  Yet, the government having the power to begin with just sets up a situation where those same evil people simply buy the power with-in the government to force people to do things against their own interests.  This is a price of unconsciousness.  It doesn't make sense and it's catastrophic.

Socialism's talking points against personal decision making and massive confiscation of people's property places it clearly far left on the field.  People typically don't stay in that area of the field for long though.  They get jobs, become parents, or observe a friend who don't work as hard complain about how little that friend has in life.  They then progress away from defending the Socialist talking points.  Later in life, most people look back on their younger ignorance with a little surprise or embarrassment. Life's pretty compelling, and it pushes people to move past these types of conversations. Older, wiser people typically encourage younger people to dig deeper because they've learned that society can't be based off theft if it's to survive.

Across the field, I place in contrast to the Socialism MOC, the Republic MOC which boasts the benefit of constitution and independence. Talking points include the acceptance that people vote on some aspects of society, but a certain set of aspects are not up for vote. An example is American's Bill of Rights and the rights and systems outlined in the Constitution.

In America, you're always free to say anything you want. Freedom of speech is noted as given to you by a creator. Thus, any attempted law or legislation designed to limit the speech of a person or punish people for speaking about prohibited ideas is null and void. America is a constitutional republic, and freedom of speech in our society is simply not up for debate. That's very different from other nations where what you say is very controlled. People in Saudi Arabia, Canada, China, England, and North Korea are regularly arrested, punished, or killed for speaking about things that their governments prohibit.

The Republic's conversations pushed towards a society that wouldn't be based off people stealing from each other. Such is outlined as property rights in the Fifth Amendment of the Constitution of the United States. Or at least that's a talking point in the Republics MOC. The MOC of the Republic is heavily rooted in the deeper MOC of Individualism, of course, and compels self-responsibility. The MOC of the Republic is the embodiment of the founding fathers who created America and the most prolific nation state in human history.

Freedom of speech and property rights were built directly in from the conversations the originators had after fighting their way out of the serfdom system of the British Collectivist Oligarchy. I didn't place it on here, but where do you think the language used to justify the system of serfdom in England belongs on the field? I'll leave that to you.

As far as the Consciousness Axis here, a speaker from the Republic MOC speaks more consciously and pushes for more individual cognition. The Republic MOC clearly iterates "Leave me alone, and I'll make my own decisions in life." The more left side notion here is the MOC of Socialism, and they aren't perfect opposites, but just track with me here. Socialism said someone else should make your decisions for you because we need to decide what is best for everyone and then force that decision on the subdued class. That's less cognition in the individual and compels less learning by the individual in life. It's a promise that you'll be protected by the collective group decisions, but nothing is off the table as far as making your personal decisions for you and your family.

The Socialism MOC speaks of protecting a person from making bad decisions for themselves. A core trade-off one must accept to speak from this area of the field is the acceptance of conceding personal control over your own life and giving up your personal self-actualization. It requires your self-actualization to be replaced with the will of someone else. The direct acceptance of Unconsciousness in all of these modalities of conversation should be taken into consideration and avoided at all cost.

This should be taken into consideration even in the modalities and conversations stemming from the right, more conscious, side of the field. Observation of consciousness and self-actualization will become *the* core aspect of life as humanity moves towards harmony. This is especially important on the left side of the field because that's where unconsciousness approaches the collapse and destruction of civilizations.

The motivation for all conversation and human effort is purely the battle between Consciousness and Unconsciousness. This is true within the individual and within society. We ultimately are responsible for society and responsible for ourselves at the same time. But we fix society by fixing ourselves. We can't legislate morals, and laws can't make you a good person. Who should make your decisions? Who should rule the city?

## The Evolution of Conversations

As you move down the field, you'll notice the prevailing phenomenon. Conversational modes are all echoes of the conversations below them. And ultimately, they're all echoes of the battle between Unconsciousness and Consciousness within the human mind. To make your own decisions and to learn slowly to make the right decisions is the battle. The Tree of Life moves against Unconsciousness in an effort to survive and maintain life as it descends into the physical plane. This effort manifests in the individual as an internal struggle to achieve self-actualization. The struggle to achieve self-actualization is what the individual is. You are the Tree's every hope and its greatest expression. You are its child. This is the nature of the Love the Tree has for You.

We within ourselves must carry the cart up the hill for life to go on. We must all confront our decision-making process as our chaotic internal battle, or we will project our tumultuous internal battle onto the Green Gift. The turmoil in the world is simply the reverberations of a being fighting to self-actualize and seeking harmony. The individual is seeking enlightenment.

You can look up the chain to see how the MOC and talking points are derived from the ones below them. And the MOC at the base are Unconsciousness and Consciousness. The modalities of conversation are all related to each other in that they are echoes of these root MOC. That's the prevailing phenomena of life. All conversations in life are the same conversation and it's a motion to become conscious.

The MOC considered to be opposites of each other are related in the way that they're inverse talking points of each other. Each one of these MOC has talking points to which the MOC opposing them will adopt and evolve counter defensive points. It's an evolutionary process of the objectification of what is actually a formless, single object... The Thing that Is. Monotheism. It's the flow of energy out of our veiled consciousness as we seek to understand ourselves. To watch God pass by from the cleft in the rock. It really is amazing and beautiful.

Each one of these archetypal modalities lived a life of its own and evolved in its own way. They developed talking points as weapons sharpened by battle with other modalities. And they developed defensive points as shields in response to attacks from other MOC.

# ~ Strata: Communism and Free Market

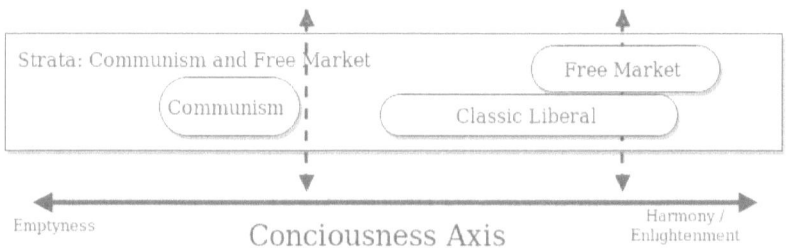

Communism ends as complete and total government control over all aspects of decision making with a promise of a resulting utopia. This narrative is typically forced on people and is the hard lesson of collectivist conversations. I'm not going to go into the perfect definition of Communism because it's a long and old conversation.

It doesn't really go anywhere to argue the definition of socialism or communism because you'll only hear "It's never been done right!" Defining Communism and even arguing for or against it isn't really the point here though. Communism's MOC strangely focuses on the idea that the source of all human suffering is that people can make their own decisions in life. It refers to this as Capitalism.

A large part of the conversation in this area of the field is denouncing any belief in a higher power because people beholden to a higher power won't fully submit their lives and will over to a ruling class. They must fear death, right? People are required to fear death to fall in line behind people speaking in the mode of Communism. Communism's talking points have no effect on people who aren't emotionally dependent on the state.

Most people accept that Karl Marx, the author of *The Communist Manifesto*, was an atheist. However, I see his creation, Communism, as a very clear belief in God as this life's work is based specifically off of hatred for God. The same disdain for God is clearly visible in modern day people who hate *What Is True*. Hatred for What Is true is of course synonymies with hating God. Karl Marx was a big part of the war against *What Is True* which predates written history and rolls on today. Communism is a war on God and Marx's contribution to the destruction of people's understanding of their purpose.

Also, in the Communist area of the field are foundational doctrines that people shouldn't raise their own children. This should sound familiar. Some even believe that it should be codified into law that children should be raised by the state as part of their Utopian dream. The promise of communist utopia is so strong in this area of the field that the people there accept that the ultimate decision makers for their family are the elite running the state. The aspiration of a family to raise and instill morals in children is the basis of humanities branch of the Tree. Derailment of that is the complete and total destruction of all order and our life on Earth. This's why the destruction of family decision making is a key aspect of the Communist MOC and all MOC derived from Communism's talking points.

I don't know how people fell for the paper thin, weaponized talking points of Communism throughout time, but it's been very successful throughout history. Communism and Socialism murdered about 80 or 200 million people in the 20th century alone. Socialism's star was Hitler, of course. Communism's greatest leaders were Trotsky, Lenin, Stalin, Mao, etc. People emotionally invested in this area of the field don't like to hear this list. Instantly you'll hear "It's never been done right!"

New ideas are rare, and our global conversations fire in predictable paths like bad habits.  I typically give people trained in the doctrines of this area of the field a chance to talk about how their ideas weren't implemented correctly.  I think it's definitely an interesting conversation, but of course, I encourage consciousness over all forms of forfeit of will.  That's my goal in life, and I feel the Communism area of conversation falls very short of that.

People speaking around the Communist MOC tend to have made an agreement with themselves that equal outcome will solve all the world's problems.  Maybe that's a straw-man of the Communist MOC, but if you have enough of these conversations, you'll find they only speak about one solution to everything.  The solution is always forced equal outcome by elites and dictators. It always requires less or no decision making by the wider population.  It always claims the answer is forcibly taking property from families and redistributing it while elites skim off the top.

The redistribution of resources in the name of equality never takes into consideration the work involved to produce those resources. For example, if factory workers feel they should own the factory, as they steal it, they never mention or speak about how hard it must have been to start the factory business from the ground up. The redefining of theft in these conversations serves as a sad coping mechanism for the abandonment of morality and honesty.

Communism is a very dangerous goal in that the population must be willing to throw away their own personal will power. They must give up the ability to make their own decisions in life. And that's the actual goal of speaking from the MOC of Communism.

Have you read *The Four Agreements* by don Miguel Ruiz? You should. Avoid the poisonous agreement that someone else should be making your decisions. The conscious reasoning for this is that we're not here to build a perfect system or some utopia to keep ourselves in line. We're not here to build the perfect state according to our temporal desires. We're not here to collect for ourselves a list of teachers and leaders to suit our selfish passions so we can wonder off into myth and extinction. We are here to build a consciousness, and that is achieved only by us *choosing* morality. Cognition! Pay attention!

Consciousness must be sought and chosen or it has no value to the long-term success of our species. This is why we internally accept that we can't legislate morals. With this, I place the Free Market as the opposite of the Communism MOC on the field. Talking points around the Free Market area speak of the inability to legislate morals. There's a lot of conversation here on personal character and making better decisions. Free Market conversations prefer a free market of ideas and compel us to seek and choose wisely as individuals.

People speaking from the Free Market MOC will often speak about the adoption of the belief that people should make their own decisions. They then should reap the fruits of their labor or face the consequences of their mistakes. Either way, society gains Conscious Capital. Capital is typically spoken about in reference to an economic system, and social capital is the gains we make towards consciousness on an individual or species level. Free markets are responsible for most great inventions and they accelerate confronting difficulties in survival like medicine and technology.

Conversations in this area of the field include people seeking what they feel is best for their lives through the decision-making process as individuals. In this process, only accepting what they feel is best for them and their families is considered to be what is best for society. By this, people floating in this area believe we'll slowly find all of the best solutions because there's incentive. Necessity is the mother of invention. This is called the profit motive in the Free Market MOC.

MOC opposing the Free Market MOC have, of course, developed defensive points such as claims that profit is a negative phenomenon and being allowed to make your own decisions is selfish. This is a good observation of the nature of opposing MOC. A counter-counter talking point here is that under Communism, there was never an incentive to create anything or make better decisions. Under Socialism, as well, there's no incentive to create anything. Without the ability to make your own decisions, the only innovative aspect of life is memorizing the entitlement structure and conforming for survival out of fear. The point here is that opposing MOC develop off each other, and the talking points volley between them quite predictably.

Under Communism the people are actually punished for supporting and producing for society. By the way, many farmers in the Soviet Union died because they owned land and were producing grain to feed the people around them. They were called Kulaks, which means greedy or miserly. Average estimates I've seen claim that the Marxist slaughtered about 6 million of the farmers they labeled Kulaks plus the resulting people who starved. The farmers grew all the food of course and famine that resulted is estimated as some at 15 million deceased. This small event alone under Communism rivaled of surpassed the death toll of Jewish Holocaust in Socialist Nazi Germany

It was called the Terror Famine, or Holodomor, and killed around twice the number of people of the entire Nazi Socialist Holocaust in Germany. It might seem on its face that they died from not having food, but in reality, they died because they wanted someone else to make their decisions for them. They selected against themselves evolutionarily. And, we might too if we ignore that fact. I encourage people to read up on the Terror Famine because it's never discussed in public education.

It's never discussed in public education because the public would be more likely to reject their children's indoctrination in grade school through college if they knew the past of communism.  Does that sound crazy?  I think it sounds crazy, but ask yourself this... Have you heard of the Holodomor?  That's no accident.

A study called the *Faculty Voter Registration in Economics, History, Journalism, Law, and Psychology* shows that Leftist account for 12 out of 13 college level professors in general and 33 out of 34 college history professors specifically.  College level professors are far beyond wanting to hide the death toll of Communism which clearly dwarfs the Holocaust.  I'm not going to get into a lot of references here though because it's not the point, and people who refuse to understand the death tolls need something else to convince them that people should make their own decisions.

On a more optimistic note, my vision is simply that we're going to move towards a time when people *will* know that they need to make their own decisions and avoid equal outcome tricks.  When you choose to let others make your decisions for you, it's no joke.

As for as the MOC of Communism, it inherited its talking points from the teaching of Karl Marx and Lenin. Marx never worked a day in his life, but being supported by extremely rich people like Friedrich Engels, decided that he would tell everyone else how to work and how to form a Utopian society to which he never contributed. Sweet!

People think of Stalin when they think about the horrors of Communism, but for some reason they don't know that it was Lennon that set up the structure of the Evil Empire and the gulags. The gulags were death camps and torture facilities. The history of the gulags is another tragedy avoided in the public education system. Read *The Gulag Archipelago* by Aleksandr Solzhenitsyn.

The George Orwell book *1984* was based off the Communist Utopia proposed by Karl Marx and properly depicts how Marx's dream would roll out in the centuries to come. North Korea, Mao China, modern day China, Nazi Germany, Communist Cambodia, Venezuela, and even Cuba. All complete failures. They oppressed and some continue to oppress masses of unconscious people speaking in the conversational modes around Communism, Socialism, and Marxism.

*1984* was about the manipulation of conversation for a reason. Changing the conversation and restricting speech is key to taking away people's ability to make their own decisions. In *1984*, all conversation was tracked and monitored. People weren't allowed to talk to each other about anything relevant. If they did, they were tortured as a trader to the collective. They weren't allowed to make any of their own decisions. In the end, the man and woman of the story who fell in love secretly where caught talking about relevant things to each other. They were forced to turn on each other through nightmarish torture and all was lost. Trust, which they'd only experienced through confiding in the other, was broken. Symbolically, the man and women were set apart from each other. The Triad was broken. Their minds were broken. Love was broken. Orwellian conversational propaganda techniques are required to collapse a society and bring on the hellish existence of unconsciousness.

A conscious and free people will stand up for themselves when they're threatened. It only takes one candle to light a completely pitch-black room. Pink

Floyd stated that "The [news] paper holds their folded faces to the floor, and every day the paper boy brings more." Buffalo Springfield said, "It starts when you are always afraid. You step out of line and man comes to take you away."

What I'm eluding to is that the failures of North Korea, Mao China, modern day China, Nazi Germany, Venezuela, Cuba, etc. are actually failures brought about by unconsciousness. It's the people's fault as they accepted unconsciousness and gave up on making their own decisions. So, pay attention! Communism is just a veneer for Unconsciousness which is people not making their own decisions. They were tricked by evil people into not being allowed to make their own decisions. This is why I graph conversations on a cognitive Consciousness Axis. That way we can see the choice to make our own decisions laid out clearly and visually. In the end, despite claiming they were tricked, they were responsible for themselves, and they paid the price for lying to themselves about that fact. People allowed to make their own decisions would never end in that way and would at least fight to the death.

Calling it Communism or Socialism only serves to communicate with those unable to understand the deeper meaning there. It's our eternal duty to pull conversations deeper and towards consciousness. What Is asks this of us. Really, the point of the whole field of conversations is to realize that all these are just modes of conversation that mask our development towards Consciousness. The real thing that killed the hundreds of millions of people in the 20th century was... Unconsciousness.

They failed to actualize Truth to themselves. They lied to themselves. They chose what was not true over What Is True and ended up walking with what is not instead of What Is. And that's a very cold path. They should've chosen to walk with What Is. It loves you and keeps you warm.

Derelict of the duty to project your will is deadly and passes through populations. The Holocaust survivor Viktor Frankl said, "The [concentration camp] prisoner who lost faith in the future – his future – was doomed. With his loss of belief in the future, he also lost his spiritual hold; he let himself decline and became subject to mental and physical decay." Read Man's Search for Meaning by Viktor Frankl and you'll understand more about this phenomenon. The same loss of spiritual hold occurs to entire nations and species. Karl Marx's war was with the Tree of Life and loss of spiritual hold was the tool he used to wilt it.

Some of these horrific events throughout history are intentional attempts by very evil people to push others into unconsciousness. Evil does exist. Wake up and demand to make your own decisions before your fate's sealed. That's the message in the wind and that's the message on the field. You either self-actualize, or you don't.

We're ready to understand our purpose now, and we'll accomplish balance. We won't collapse into another dark age this time. The experiment succeeds this time because we see now and have the right communication tools. We're ready this time, and we'll reject unconsciousness in our day to day lives. With gratitude, we'll demand to make our own decisions and be responsible while understanding the reasons behind morality. Morality is required for the survival of our species.

It could be said that some people were tricked into letting others make their decisions for them, but in the end, they knew deep down inside as do you and I. They were warned by family, society, loved ones, every nature show they watched, their Bible, life in general, and the very wind itself.

On this rock, you are your own advocate. I'll be your advocate as well. I love you for reasons that you do not yet understand. It's why I'm doing this. But I digress. Back to the field, the next strata is a little bit more abstract.

## ~ Strata: The State

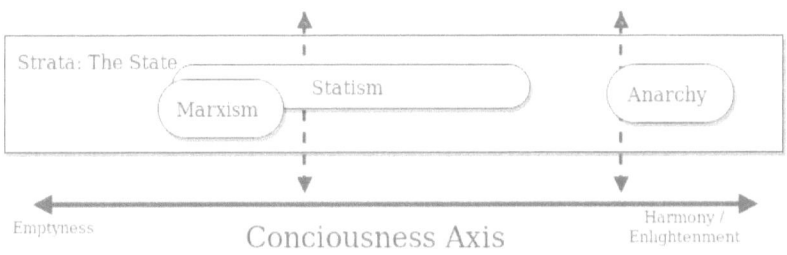

I placed the MOC of Anarchy towards the right side of the field. Conversations around the Anarchy area of the field are always interesting and fun. They're like loops of formlessness and avoidance of rules. People here float around making up their own mind on societal structure. This would take a large amount of individual discipline to work on a large scale but will be approached as people become more conscious.

Anarchy conversations have always been strange to me because they speak of anarchy as a social structure that could be adopted to avoid the enumerable problems with the state. Yet a pure society like a working anarchy could never be adopted per se. But I do believe that people approach anarchy as they become enlightened and conscious. But Anarchy would never be adopted, it would only be arrived at.

So why do these people keep talking about adopting anarchy?

They should just talk about consciousness and deeper conversations about the Green Gift and know that we'll end up where we should be. Adopting the peace required for Anarchy is a great concept. But really, I feel like the advocates neither understand what they're talking about nor have a clue as to how to achieve it. Eventually these people will adopt this field MOC philosophy and help push humanity towards the balance they are seeking. Speaking about this field of conversations is a mode of conversation itself. It's my preferred mode of conversation although I can basically step into any of the others.

The MOC of Anarchy is a pretty good candidate to oppose Marxism/Communism MOC. However, it doesn't depict the highest moral or spiritual status. It doesn't ascribe to a power outside of itself and that turns out to be very important to the long-term survival of life on this plane of existence. We have to place faith in something outside of ourselves long term because a human isn't capable of producing a logical defense for concepts like our right to survive, purpose, or morals.

We require belief in a higher power to believe in something like purpose. That becomes apparent if you loop the question why? why? why? to any stance like "I should be allowed to live." Ask a friend if they should be allowed to live and keep asking why to whatever they respond with. At some point, as they're defending their stance, they must just say, "That's what I believe, and I don't have to defend it to anyone. Because I can't." The why? why? why? exposes this very quickly.

Like the previous example, all stances in life, big or small, follow the intrinsic assumption that they can't be logically defended. Faith is required at the point of surrender to this fact. Faith is defined as belief without proof. And the faith that there is a greater plan is required to confidently say that you actually should be allowed to live. A higher power must hold that plan. Our minds actually don't work without the belief in a higher power.

Anarchy's MOC rarely pulls conversations into the realm of faith or gratitude for what we've been given. It rarely pulls a person towards *The Thing That Is* or conversations around a higher power. With this, Anarchy shoots just short of Consciousness.

Avoidance of faith also gives it the flaw of talking about how humans can derive morals. This is why Anarchy, the lawless state, can't be adopted. It can only be arrived at through Consciousness and surrender to *The Thing that Is*. It can only be arrived at slowly through time. And at that point, it's more gracious just to call it Consciousness and not Anarchy. So, the word Anarchy is a total miss. But it's interesting to talk about.

But yes, a perfectly enlightened group of humans who understand *What Is*, will be very Anarchic in that they'll not require a state or laws. After all, people don't simply allow others around them to live specifically because there are laws against murder. People want others to live long, healthy lives because of an intrinsic understand of the value of life. And mentally ill people who are incapable of evoking empathy can kill without reflection despite the word of the law. That is to say that, to some degree, the laws against murder, while necessary now, really don't have as much effect on our day to day life as some would say. The people around you are conscious enough to avoid killing you. Overall, conversations around Anarchy are very interesting.

The definition of Anarchy is very nebulous. It's hard to place on the field, but its mode of conversation does have distinct talking points and Utopian goals. It definitely is on the more conscious side of the field of conversation where people make their own decisions. Especially so when compared to the talking points and defensive points of Marxism's MOC. Anarchists are all about making their own decisions, and they don't want to be told what to do. They approach Consciousness.

## ~ Strata: Collectivism and Individualism

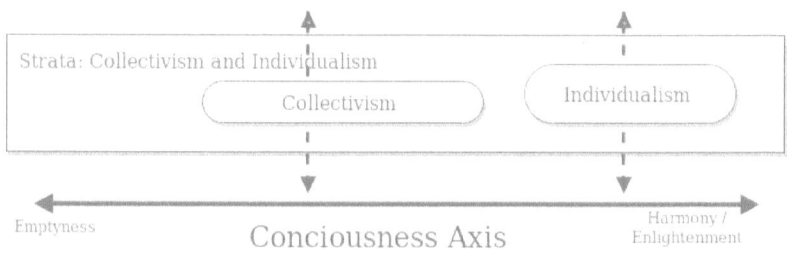

One strata lower contains conversations on which you won't, in modern times, hear people speak commonly. These are older philosophical conversations that people talked about for the last thousands of years. However, you can of course see their echoes clearly today. Plato dealt with these ideas as he spoke of "Who should rule the city?" and what he called the Organic State. Not super important other than to note this is an old conversation and talking points derived therein are quite established. We rarely get the chance to dig down deeper into these philosophies, but they're the basis of many of our society's psychological structure. Here are pivotal conversations which heavily impact the future of humanity. The two MOC here are known as the Collectivism MOC and the Individualism MOC. They are great examples of symbiotic opposites.

There are many videos and discussions online on the battle between Collectivism and Individualism. I would suggest to anyone to sit down for a week or a month and watch every video you can find on the battle between these philosophical MOC. The way you do anything is the way you do everything. Your answer to the question "Who should rule the city?" will be the same answer you'll have to the question "Who should rule your mind?" So, before you attempt those questions, accept that your purpose here is to self-actualize against all odds.

This strata is important because its talking points are on the edge of divine consciousness yet still concrete enough to heavily influence the Political strata. These conversations edge on the divine because they directly deal with the question of "Should you utilize your own will, or should you succumb to the will of others?" It's a raw question whose answer brings the validity of your existence directly into question and is reflective of your fundamental self-respect. It doesn't get much simpler than that y'all, and you're not talking your way out of it.

Collectivism's conversational mode speaks about how we should view ourselves as a group of people, and decisions should be made by a collective. The entity making the decisions for the collective can be anything from a democracy to a dictatorship, and everything in between not including individual, personal will. Individualism's conversational mode is focused on achieving individual autonomy to make decisions. It recognizes that people are the part of creation that makes decisions. It's embodied by a push for personal responsibility and refinement of human will.

"Liberate the minds of men, and ultimately you will liberate the bodies of men." - Marcus Garvey

The enemy of collectivism is the individual being able to make independent decisions. Making your own decisions is labeled selfish. The enemy of Individualism is the inevitable group of elites abusing others and making selfish decisions. You can see how the basic conversational battles in this strata echo upward into other conversations and into basic social policy. Some people want to be left alone, and some people won't leave them alone.

The Collectivism MOC of course goes on the left side of the field as it reduces the will of the individual and stifles consciousness. The Individualism MOC goes more to the right side of the field because it values will power and self-actualization. Collectivism destroys social capital, and Individualism builds social capital. This is a big area of the field so I'll leave it at that for now. There is no shortage of talking points here.

This strata is amazing. It gives a strong base on which to see the roots and reasoning behind some upper, shallower MOC. This is a great point to start looking upwards through the field. From here, you can clearly start to see how the conversations stacked on each other thought out time.

Remember, we always try to speak *with* people and identify *with* people first on whatever level they're currently speaking from. Then we try to pull them deeper and towards consciousness. Understanding these deeper conversations of Collectivism and Individualism helps in that pull. Pull slowly but surely. Be fluid.

"Be like water." - Bruce Lee

## Looking Down and Looking Up

It's only when you're in a shallower area toward the top like the Democrat MOC or the Republican MOC that you look down and everything looks confusing. One reason to go into deeper conversations is the fact that deeper conversations more clearly display why to move right towards consciousness. A good example of this is if you understand how to speak strongly from the mode of Individualism, you'll understand the roots of the MOC of Libertarianism. You'll more robustly be able to defend and speak on the talking points associated with Free Markets. Your momentum and resolve will be naturally stronger because you're speaking simpler talking points from a much deeper mental stance. You'll also understand why the Republic was formed, and you'll understand the Revolutionary War from a deeper level, and why Conservatives act the way they do. You'll be able to understand the invisible basis of the talking points above. You'll know how to articulate more nuanced answers to complex questions when speaking from shallower MOC if you have an understanding of the deeper ones. The pull to the right, while in deeper conversation, is a bit easier to rationalize as conscious cognition always trumps unconscious slumber. The deeper your conversation is pulled, the more obvious it becomes that all conversation in general is a veiled battle between consciousness and unconsciousness.

In that same way, if you speak strongly from the modality of Collectivism, you'll naturally be much more able to articulate strongly the approach of Carl Marx and navigate a wider set of difficult questions around Communism and Socialism. Similarly, if you're versed in Marxist Doctrine, you'll be a much more efficient speaker in the conversations around the Democrat area of the field. Naturally people grow out of the MOC on the left side of the field as they ultimately aren't defensible in their unconscious roots. The theory of strength though deeper understanding is the same, though.

Understanding the talking points of a deeper root of a conversation will make you a stronger speaker when speaking from a shallower echo of that conversation. Someone who doesn't understand the conversational mode of Collectivism will have a weaker ability to defend the Democratic party in conversation. Also, someone who has never looked into or read through conversations from the mode of Individualism will have a harder time defending the Republic and Free Markets. This is because a person restricted to shallow conversation can only go so deep. Escapism and entertainment limit depth in this way and are dangerous as they can be used paint a civilization into a corner.

Deeper understandings create stronger resolve, and this is true of all conversations derived from deeper MOC. It's important to note that there aren't modes or talking points deeper than the strata of Pure Consciousness. There are no deeper notions on which to base agreements or decisions made in the strata of Pure Consciousness. All agreements and all decisions here require faith and vision.

## The Formation of the Columns

Communism naturally rolled out of the theories that Marx and his buddies defined. Again, as an observation of the field, you can see the link between Communism's talking points and the conversational stance of Socialism. Also, in this derivative chain you can see the development of the political left side conversations in America, Canada, and Europe. You can see the relation to the Democratic Party in America clearly on the left side of the field.

Also, in that same way, you can see the point of the conversations around Individualism and see directly how they translate through time to echo up the right side of the field. Individualism's talking points are more or less manifested in the Republic, which embodies free markets, freedom of speech, freedom to make your own decisions in life, Capitalism, and the free market of ideas in general. Some other people openly speak against free speech and want to regulate by force, fine, imprisonment, and even death the things others are allowed to say and think. This is warworthy and that war has actually already started.

Some foreshadowing... the dichotomy of these two columns manifesting in the field is itself an echo of the base phenomena of life which is the dichotomy of Unconsciousness and Consciousness. To be or not to be? Consciously you or unconsciously someone else, who gets to make your decisions in life? You can see how this naturally translates into shallower manifestations of consciousness up through the Libertarian mode of conversation and the classical American approach to life with conversations around the Constitution. Many of these notions are specifically written in the American Constitution itself as the freedom of speech and property rights.

Leftist talking points loop disdain for the Constitution and anything related to American values because of they are echoes of Unconsciousness. The freedoms to make your own decisions and raise your own children are the bedrock of the Conservative MOC, and this is clearly an echo of Consciousness. To be!

Point being, now that we are looking from a deeper conversational strata the shallower echoes up top look much clearer and can be defended and articulated much more clearly. Also, you see the dichotomy of pro-consciousness and anti-consciousness echoed in the conversations above. The shallower the conversation, the more you'll notice petty infighting which only promises frustration and tragedy. Dig deeper to move to the right side of the field. It's simply amazing!

## ~ Strata: Religion and Spirituality

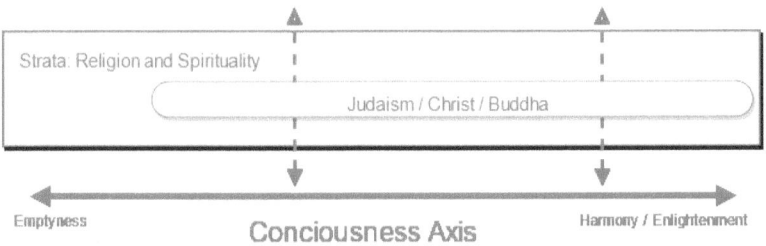

I only placed three MOC on this field as examples in this strata. This is because people who either understand or don't understand specific religions will see them in different locations on the field. Conversations posed by the brave and rare people who choose to speak from this strata approach the edge of human conversation. They are by far the most interesting people to me. Each religion or spiritual teaching has talking points typically brought forth by ancient texts or teachings of some sage. Many of the conversations in this area have common themes of enlightenment and human development.

Also, I have to put a quick disclaimer here. Differentiate these three things. There is a difference between oppressive dogma, simple dogma that helps scaffold the minds of children, and the true meaning of what ancient texts are representing. No person can separate those concepts for you, and you're definitely on your own to seek what's true in life. I say this in response to people saying things like "Do you really believe that a man lived in the stomach of a whale?" Something is being missed there.

No human can show another human the perfect map to enlightenment. I will say though that self-actualization can definitely only come from self-reflection and observations within. The texts and traditions are simply to let you know that you're not alone in your journey and that humans for thousands or millions of years have walked this path. And on that path, they saw and learned the same things and they want you to know that.

If you can't sift out positive teachings from religions text, dig deeper and you might find what you're looking for. If you have disdain for religion or spirituality and that's blocking you from seeking through ancient texts, no one can help you there. My suggestion is to avoid fishing into the fire. There are no fish there! I hope you'll join me one day. I dug for decades, and I believe I've found what I was looking for. The metaphors I found in ancient text let me know I was on the right path as I sought truth within myself.

I feel like I can look back at the childish dogma I walked through so far with admiration and see how I didn't understand it fully when I first heard it. I keep in mind when reading ancient texts that there really are two planes of existence. I had to dig pretty hard to get through a jungle of dogma, confusion, and surface level contradiction to reach the beach on the other side. Two roads diverge, my friend, and our choices make all the difference.

But I digress. I'll continue this conversation around the MOCs of Religion and Spirituality without negativity for dogma. I just want to talk about the religions that I enjoy and from which I've had a positive influence. I put Judaism, Christianity, and Buddhism on the chart here. As you can see, I put them farther to the right side because I've experienced them as overwhelming forces of consciousness in my life. Their consciousness is their gift to me. I could also put Don Miguel Ruiz, Eckhart Tolle, Don Juan, etc., on this field too, but I'm keeping this example arrangement simple. Also, I see more consciousness in some than others.

The religions I placed on the field are towards the consciousness side relative to some other modalities. Anarchy, in its arrival and less its approach, is out there. Free Market economics is out there as it's the physical expression of free will as an economic system, which is quite beautiful and relevant. I put Judeo-Christian stances and modalities of conversation way out right because of the Ten Commandments which are ultimately big, big keys to seeking the truth in life and walking with *What Is*. The Commandments, as strange as it may sound to some, have turned out to be a major force of Free Will and self-actualization for me. They are quite close to a pure truth and a pretty straight arrow towards long term harmony on The Green Gift.

The conversation within Judaism's belief that everything is one thing, Mono-Theism, is humanity's core statement and fountain of self-reflection and enlightenment. Everything is one thing. Not that Jews solely own this concept, but the conversations in their area of the field definitely embody Mono-Theism which is central to existence. I'll skip a long and disappointing conversation at this point by simply saying that Jews aren't immune to walking away from their purpose.

There's also a lot to be taken from the stories of Abraham, Moses, and many of the other Biblical characters. I'll leave that for you though. As strange as it sounds, I can open the Old Testament, and nine times out of ten, the page I open to will tell me something shockingly applicable to whatever is stressing me that day. I've been amazed so many times.

Judaism, as a root of morality, is a central core of conversations in the religious strata of Americans and Europeans continuing straight up the right side of the field of conversation. If you're from the West, Judaism's conversation is echoed in basically every conversation you've had in your life whether you understand how or not. It's axiomatic to human communication in the West at this point.

The origin of the Ten Commandments also seems like a miracle to me. It's is an eye-opening conversation in itself. These conversations are very old, and there's nothing new under the Sun. Conversations based off the Ten Commandments seem more galvanized. Morality isn't for the sake of being nice. It's required for existence. The moralities denoted in the Commandments were given to a people who could never fathom how applicable the Commandments would be for thousands of years to come.

I really have a fondness of Christianity as well in America conversation. The understanding of the phenomena of the second coming is truly more amazing than I would have imagined before I started looking into it in detail. I love talking with people who can speak strongly from a Christian stance because conversation in this area of the field is still capable of highlighting a higher power when other conversations have abandoned faith.

Faith in a higher power turns out to be important logistically for life because it provides for a person the ability to opt out of the dominance hierarchy of man. "Critical" is what must be said here! Opt out of the dominance hierarchy of man as soon as possible. The Path of stepping out of the hierarchy of man, surrendering to What Is, forming the Triad, and joining the crystalline nature of existence (the Tree of Life), turns out to *BE* consciousness/self-actualization. And that action *IS* the unfolding of kingdom in the mind and on Earth. Sounds wild, right? That Path isn't new, and as they say, there is nothing new under the Sun.

The challenge to each human is resistance to being part of the Tree of Life by catering to the person's proclivity to be off the mark and succumb to unconsciousness. John B. Calhoun called the extreme of this first death. The conversations around first and second deaths are fascinating! Choose rebirth and Second Life instead. Soon life on Earth will unfold as we go through the conversations to reach that harmony, and this will correspond with a personal unfolding in your mind along that path.

Read about his rat experiments if you haven't. He put a bunch of rats together and gave them unnaturally unlimited food and resources. They all ended up going insane and dying. I see this being because they stopped focusing on the Tree of Life. They stole, they didn't value family structure, they killed each other, and their minds shattered. And in continuing experiments, he couldn't get a rat whose mind reached this point to ever recover. Something inside them broke forever. It turns out that rats don't live by bread and water alone either.

It's time to dig deep. The elation of traveling that path is referred to as building the Kingdom within and once there, you'll innately start to build a similar Kingdom in physical plane. We'll do so with arms fueled by gratitude, free will, and no outside force will be required to compel us. No state!

That's all a bit meta and fluffy for some. I understand and that's okay. I don't seek to convince. I seek to say what I've been asked to say. I want you to know, as you see it forming, that you're not alone and you never were. It really is an amazing time to live. All types of conversations I've had in this area of the field seem to echo life, gratitude, love for the Green Gift, and *The Thing That Is*. The Religious strata is a dance around the notion of the divine and beautiful to those who are seekers.

## Where I Float

People focusing on this area of the field really can carry on life on Earth for an extended period of time where as people aligned by other conversations will crumble. Understanding this, existence and consciousness can be looked at as symbiotes or just synonyms. Amazing stuff here. To be! I really am thankful for the gift I've been given, and see it as my duty therein to hover in this area of conversation as much as possible. The breath of life has been placed in our lungs to be released back out of our mouths once we become grateful and once we receive the gift.

I'm sure that sounds like crazy talk to some but not to all. The time is upon us. Life existed to produce harmony and there's nothing like a message whose time has come. Welcome to the present!! There's no time like it. Seize the day! What are you waiting for? A certain shade of green? Those who control the past control the future, and those who control the present control the past. Enough crazy talk for now. You either know what I'm talking about or you soon will.

## Other Religions

The other religions fit on the field as well. All conversation can be mapped to the field. All talking points are on the field somewhere. If you're a math person then just picture the field as the super set domain of all possible concepts you can declare or agree to. They clump together in modes.

I won't rationalize my placement of Buddhism here, but great conversations happen in the area of Buddhism. There are many Indian philosophical conversations in this strata as well that I won't approach in this quick analysis of the field. The word Jihad is also a reference to the internal struggle of the individual as part of the Tree of Life's actualization. We self-reflect on as many conversations in the field as possible to sharpen ourselves. I just really like Judeo-Christian stuff.

## ~ Strata: Pure Consciousness

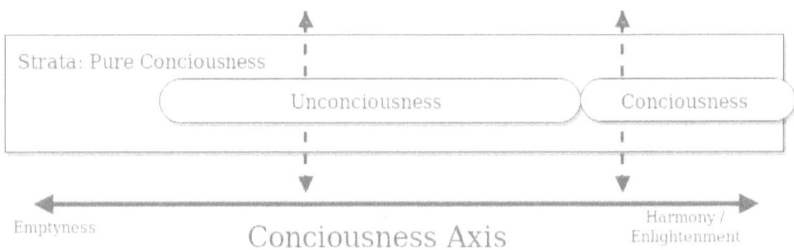

Understanding the next strata requires looking at the modes and how they interact with each other. This strata has two different modes of conversation which are so abstract they are almost not applicable to this plane of existence, yet they are. They're difficult to formulate coherent conversations around, and they're difficult to reason on with words. But I will anyway. This strata is the MOC of Unconsciousness and MOC of Consciousness. The MOC of Consciousness is the path to the Kingdom. Conversations in this strata may revolve around the basic truths and axioms of reality such as

- You should express your will
- You should not express your will
- You should fight to survive

- Survival is valueless
- You have the right to defend your family
- You do not have the right to defend your family
- You should not have a family
- You should have family
- You should not be allowed to raise your own children
- You should be allowed to raise your own children
- You do not have the right to exist
- You have the right to exist
- The world is a bad place
- The world is a good place

## To Be or Not to Be

This strata is very "To be or not to be." That is the question here. And, as all strata and modes of conversation echo upwards, "To be or not to be" is actually the question at every strata of conversation. Every conversation attempts the question "To be or not to be". It is The Question. Reciprocally, every statement is an attempt to answer this question. It's the only question and every statement is simply one of two answers to that question.

A choice to be is why you practice to win the hockey game. It's why we want to visit the Moon. It's why you feel the way you do when you look in your newborn's eyes. This is the strata of conversation where self-actualization lies open and is the focus of the conversation whereas the focus on self-actualization in other strata of conversation is merely echoed but present. This is the strata where you finally ask yourself if you should be or if you should not be. It's either terrifying or it's beautiful.

Helen Keller said it best. "Life is either a daring adventure or nothing." This is one of many iconic quotes from her book appropriately named *Let Us Have Faith* published in 1940.

## Simplicity of Consciousness

Consciousness is very simply making cognitive decisions, making choices, living in the now, and attempting to survive. Notice I said attempting. People naturally make what they think is the best decision relative to the maintaining of their life, finding purpose, and providing for their future. Unconsciousness is avoidance, escapism, deferring decision-making, and letting others decide our fate. Unconsciousness is feeling like everything is Zen, and we are passively watching life.

Unconscious conversations are reactive to an adverse world that burdens us. Conscious conversations are proactive in a complimentary world that sharpens us. I seek, of course, proactive consciousness because I've grown to love *What Is* and want it to go on. I want this to go on forever! I accept its offer of eternal life, and I'm grateful. I compel *It* to go on by observing *It* openly and promoting what *It* loves. I am Connectedness, strategic, activation, woo, communication.

# Reflection on the Field

## The Pillars Above

You can see how these two basic modalities of conversation formulate the pillars of modalities above them all the way up to entertainment. All of the shallower MOC areas are nebulously morphing into each other yet all based off this fundamental, low level strata. So, the Unconsciousness and Consciousness strata is important to the top/bottom Complexity Axis in that it informs the modalities above it.

Consciousness is recognizing that you're alive. The upper realm of consciousness is to see further and be thankful to *The Thing That Is*. Consciousness is the recognition of *The Thing That Is* for reasons we'll spend forever reflecting on. Consciousness is the recognition of the Spiral nature of life. The Spiral being the relationship between man and woman. The Yin and the Yang.

Consciousness' application turns out to lead to a point where one desires to put energy into the triad of the father, the mother, and the child because that's the crystalline nature of the Tree of Life. The crystalline nature of life is one of my favorite concepts to talk about. It's Beautiful. More specifically, it's what beauty is.

## Hot and Cold Water

An interesting observation of the Unconsciousness and Consciousness strata is that you're never really unconscious. You're only thinking less or letting someone else partially think for you. If you're not thinking at all, you would die or not exist. Your brain requires activity to make your heart beat, to feed yourself, and put your pants on.

Think of two glasses of water. There's hot water, and there's cold water. There's such a thing as heat. But there's actually no such thing as cold. Scientifically and physically, there's no such thing as cold. Cold is an adjective applied to an object with less heat. But it has heat, just less heat. There's something with more heat in it, and we call it hot water. And, there's something with less heat in it, and we call it cold water. But they both have heat in them.

Consciousness is the same way. There is no unconscious. There's only less consciousness, and we build it as an energy in our mind, in our plight, and in our behavior. In our self-reflection and our ability to manifest reality, we exercise and build that confidence in our being. This power/energy is called Consciousness. It's an energy like heat. It's an energy like any other energy and it flows. It's like a ball of energy that's stored in us that we release in the form of focused will towards our survival. The activation of our will is the flowering of our consciousness.

See how concepts in this area of the field are more difficult to word and more difficult to reason on? But it's fun, right? People will begin to talk more in this strata, and the tumultuous nature of our time is the indicator that people are ready and thirsty. They seek to make their own decisions in life.

Again, to bring it back into more practical terms, will power is an actual physical energy that you use to pick up spoons, to eat food, to build a fence, and to drive to work. Self-reflection and the choice to self-actualize drives you to fulfillment or harmony. That's your plight and purpose. We are to move towards greater Consciousness as we go through time. We are to move towards the greater human destiny. We're to challenge ourselves and accept responsibility for ourselves as we grow. We build the Kingdom inside, begin to walk with What Is, and then build the Kingdom in the Green Gift physically with focused will.

We're not always going to make the right decisions of course, but we do need to be making our own decisions. We're ready for self-actualization. Especially if we're wild enough to still be tuned in to this conversation. Let's just say, we're more interesting than we let on to others. We both know that. The more consciousness we wield and the more decisions we're making for ourselves, the more we as a species can exert our will Power for larger and larger goals. We have very large challenges, and we will rise to them as we experience the Green Gift. I am human, you will hear me roar.

I am the Passion; I am The Warfare. I will never stop... always constant, accurate, and intense.     - Steve Vai

## Stepping Back

When you step back from a conversation, you'll see beyond your own agreements, which are typically difficult to defend. You'll see the raw struggle of animalistic survival. We mask it with personality. This personality is not you, and the talking points you end up adopting don't fully define you. They can and will change throughout time. So, in this light, it becomes useful to notice the pattern of adoption of talking points and modes of speaking to yourself and to the world.

I always push downward into the deep and right toward consciousness. Also, keep in mind that as sure as you may not be fully represented by the mode of conversation you are speaking from, the person you are talking to may not be fully represented by the mode of conversation they're speaking from. You may not be talking to the person at all actually. You're typically just interfacing with the mode of conversation they're speaking from as they try talking points on you. They're ironing out the whys and moving through the adoption of conversational modes as well.

In a way, you may never actually speak to anyone. It might be more accurate to say we merely tap on the glass of someone's experience when we speak to them, and lord knows what they really hear. It's like two ships passing in the night. Life is actually just one long conversation, and it's a conversation you have with yourself. I want us enjoy it.

This is also why many people simply end up preaching only to their choir and why it sometimes seems like people aren't listening to us. They are simply using the modes of conversation they're accustomed to, and it's not about being right or wrong. They're simply defending the stance they believe is securing them in that moment and communication isn't really occurring. Remember, it's not our job to convince anyone of anything, but it is our job to recognize patterns inside ourselves and become more on the mark.

## The Mode of You

So, what should I call the specific collection of talking points that I've amassed and experimented with? If the ego and these temporal modes of speaking don't really represent me, then who am I? And isn't that an old question?  Well, *I am Who I Am*.  Does that sound familiar?  I am part of *What Is* and that's the best description I'll find here.  Yet that question being answered doesn't stop the show.  And I'm glad it doesn't.  *What Is* is everything, and that includes me.  I am a part of it.  There's nothing new being said here.  Accepting this, I personally don't perfectly fit into any one of the archetypal conversation stances on the field and neither do you.  You and I are combinations of some of the MOC and random talking points.

Accordingly, few people will label themselves as a simple subscriber to any archetypal mode.  And sports fans aren't ever simply sports fans.  The actual place on the field to which my exact stance is mapped is called... me.  Mine is called Samuel.  Samuel is just another one of the modes of conversation.  A set of talking points and a conversation flow.  After all, the real me is just a man on the land.  I'm just a guy you passed on the road.  I'm just enjoying my time in the cleft In the rock.  I asked for proof of God, and This is what It showed me.

## Your Current Modality

Why did I lay this field out?  Why look at the modalities in the field and try to see how they're interacting with each other rather than getting really proficient at one certain modality and being contented with being strong there?  The reason is that staying in one modality can be a trap of ego and doesn't fulfill my purpose.

But as a Devil's advocate, wouldn't it be easier just to pick one modality and memorize all its talking points and defensive points.  Then I could use those talking points and defensive points in all scenarios in such a way, so efficiently, that no one could ever win an argument against me.  This would be a static approach to life and people.

For example, I could know all the talking points within the doctrine of Communism.  I could spout on and on about all the writings and historical events pertaining to the proletariat.  I could talk endlessly about the ways that past events could have gone differently.  It's never been done right!!!  No one I know could talk me out of how great Communism is because I had spent so much time invested, personally and emotionally, in speaking from that mode. I could believe that it benefits me personally to stay there because I basically could always consider myself to be right. I'd feel safe there. I could use the conversation to get what I need from those around me. Why would I ever zoom out and look at other modalities as interacting archetypal conversational modes? Why analyze the interaction of the modalities in general, rather than simply speaking from the modality in which I'm currently well versed?

Well, analyzing the modalities and the interaction on this level is the point of the field. By stepping back and seeing how the modalities interact, I can see how people interact. I can see that people aren't really any of these modalities, even when they think they are. The modalities set up the talking points, they set up the defensive points, and the people act out the scene. It's a theater of fear. It's Plato's cave.

To see the modalities allows a person to predict the behavior of others. Some of the modalities are even designed and pushed specifically to control the behavior of their zealots. The nature of unconsciousness is the tail wagging the dog. Studying the field allows a person to see straight through the things people are saying and into the drive of mankind.

Seeking this is where our minds belong because our goal is greater human destiny and to reflect on ourselves. This is so we can experience ourselves and enjoy ourselves in the green gift. The man at the river knows the answers to your questions.

The Free Market speakers want strong economy for reasons they may not even fully understand themselves. They believe the economy is the core of society and civilization, and they're mostly right. Some people identify as Republicans because they want to save America, or whatever other core opinion in which they've emotionally invested. The people involved in Socialist conversations believe that the safety net is paramount to long term harmony, and that says something about their journey in life. People adopting modes around Marxism truly believe that the problems in the world stem from the profit motive. The MOC of Statism is similar. Collectivism's MOC is the source there. Modes of Individualism iterate the development of negative rights as the basis of harmony. All these modalities are adopted along with a hope for the benefits they're perceived to offer. To step back and look at the field and how the modes interact is to truly understand the fabric of society.

When we step back, we can see how all the conversations are weaving together and why people are emotionally investing in their stances. My goal, by uncovering the ways these modalities have evolved and are related, is to show that there is a Free Market of ideas here. Beautifully enough, if we can offer someone something better, society will switch modes and focus on its long-term movement through the field. There is a greater philosophical offer here. Always push conversations deeper, towards consciousness, and people making their own decisions. I want to see people move beyond any stagnant conversations they're stuck in and towards something greater. And I'm happy to tell you, Consciousness is king, ladies and gentlemen!

Be Brave!

> Let them hear the breath of life.
>
> It's time.
>
> Wake the Lion.

www.ingramcontent.com/pod-product-compliance
Lightning Source LLC
Chambersburg PA
CBHW021126080526
44587CB00010B/654